COGNITIVE DEVELOPMENTAL THERAPY WITH CHILDREN

COGNITIVE DEVELOPMENTAL THERAPY WITH CHILDREN

Tammie Ronen

The Bob Shapell School of Social Work, Tel Aviv University, Israel

JOHN WILEY & SONS

Chichester · New York · Weinheim · Brisbane · Singapore · Toronto

Other Wiley Editorial Offices

John Wiley & Sons, Inc., 605 Third Avenue,
New York, NY 10158-0012, USA

VCH Verlagsgesellschaft, Pappelallee 3,
0-69469 Weinheim, Germany

Jacaranda Wiley Ltd, 33 Park Road, Milton,
Queensland 4064, Australia

John Wiley & Sons (Asia) Pte Ltd, 2 Clementi Loop #02-01,
Jin Xing Distripark, Singapore 129809

John Wiley & Sons (Canada) Ltd, 22 Worcester Road,
Rexdale, Ontario M9W 1L1, Canada

Library of Congress Cataloging-in-Publication Data

British Library Cataloguing in Publication Data

A catalogue record for this book is available from the British Library

ISBN 0-471-97006-9 (cased)
ISBN 0-471-97007-7 (paper)

Typeset in 11/13pt Palatino from the author's disks by Dorwyn Ltd, Rowlands Castle, Hampshire
Printed and bound in Great Britain by Antony Rowe Ltd, Eastbourne

This book is printed on acid-free paper responsibly manufactured from sustainable forestation, for which at least two trees are planted for each one used for paper production.

To my daughters, Efrat and Anat, with love

*They were my best teachers in child development
and challenged me every day to practise
what I advised my clients*

CONTENTS

ABOUT THE AUTHOR

Dr Tammie Ronen is a senior lecturer at the Bob Shapell School of Social Work at Tel Aviv University. She is the author of four books in Hebrew on self-control with children, helping parents in educating children for self-control, children's disorders and cognitive therapy. She has published over 30 papers in the area of cognitive therapy and children. In addition to her full-time position at the university, she is very active in her clinic in treating children and parents with cognitive therapy. Dr Ronen is the president of the Israeli Association for Cognitive and Behavioural Therapies.

Dr Tammie Ronen has given many workshops on cognitive developmental therapy with children in Israel, Europe and the United States.

ACKNOWLEDGEMENTS

This book is an outcome of many years of treating children and lecturing in the area of child intervention and cognitive therapy. I would genuinely like to thank my students from the School of Social Work and the School of Education at Tel Aviv University, who urged me to translate my ideas into one theoretical framework for assessment and intervention.

I would also like to express my true appreciation to Michael Coombs of John Wiley, who accompanied me from the very beginning of this journey, from early discussions on the idea of writing this book, and all the way through to its completion.

To the Bob Shapell School of Social Work—my second home during the last decade—I would like to express my gratitude for its financial and spiritual support of my writing, enabling its publication.

I must also relay my deep appreciation to those stimulating children who have come to me for therapy and who have clarified my understanding of developmental processes while inspiring my pursuit of the optimal means for reaching out to children in need.

And last, but certainly not least, I would like to thank Dee B. Ankonina for her enterprising and demanding editing. Through our years of working together, Dee, a clinical child psychologist, has become a friend and a collaborator in bringing my writings to fruition.

FOREWORD
By AARON BECK

The impact of cognitive therapy has been world wide. Various therapists who have received training in the United States, Britain, and Europe have spread out all over the world so that there are now cognitive therapists in most of the developing as well as the developed countries. It is, to me, particularly gratifying to know that cognitive therapy has established a strong foothold in Israel and that distinguished clinicians and scholars, such as Tammie Ronen the author of this volume, have expanded the frontiers of cognitive therapy to include children.

Since the development of cognitive therapy over thirty years ago there has been an increasing refinement of procedures and a broadening of the significant basis for this approach to psychiatric disorders. As more highly trained and experienced therapists have utilised the cognitive therapy approach, its application has been expanded to a wide variety of disorders and also to different populations. Cognitive therapists have developed and tested various forms of cognitive therapy for almost every psychiatric disorder. Among those problems in which the efficacy of cognitive therapy has been demonstrated are depression, anxiety disorders, panic, obsessive–compulsive disorder, post-traumatic stress disorder, and the various eating disorders. Cognitive therapy has also been shown to be helpful in the treatment of the personality disorders, including borderline personality disorder. Two studies have shown its efficacy in the treatment of heroin addicts and two studies have demonstrated its efficacy in the treatment of cocaine addiction.

Cognitive therapy has also been shown to be effective with a wide variety of demographic variables: it has been effective with people with high as well as low intellectual functioning; with children and youth as well as the geriatric population; with poorly educated as well as well educated; and with the socially and economically deprived, as well as affluent populations. It has been proved to be a valuable component of marital therapy, group therapy, and family therapy.

The volume *Cognitive Developmental Therapy with Children* presents a model for child intervention. For many years, cognitive therapy has been considered inappropriate for children due to their concrete way of thinking and limited ability to deal with abstract concepts. This book emphasises the feasibility of cognitive therapy with children and demonstrates that children can learn, enjoy, and benefit from cognitive intervention. The book constitutes an attempt to bring together several features and orientations: a developmental–educational approach, cognitive therapy, and basic treatment principles used with children.

Although a number of studies have been reported on the use of cognitive therapy with children, most of them tended to focus either on the conditions that induce children to change their thoughts (i.e., behavioural techniques for teaching children different ways of thinking) or on the use of a single technique such as self-instruction or self-talk. Other studies used common therapeutic methods (such as play therapy) in order to change children's dysfunctional cognitions. The underlying message of this volume is that cognitive therapy can be used with children following the same principles that guide adult therapy, but gearing it to the children's level of cognitive development. Children, like adults, can be taught to identify their negative automatic thoughts, to understand the thought–emotion relationship, and to develop a more functional way of thinking.

The volume presents a comprehensive theory for understanding children's behaviour, linking together the 'three legs of therapy': assessment, intervention, and evaluation. It describes cognitive therapy as a continuous process of therapeutic decisions that are based on the specific characteristics of each child's ways of thinking and his or her dysfunctional cognitions. Particular emphasis is put on the role of emotions in the development and maintenance of psychological disorders as well as on the crucial role they play in the process of change. A good therapist–child relationship will enable the child to deal with difficult emotions while being able to accept painful emotions and to express both positive and negative emotions.

The first part of the book describes the unique features of childhood disorders and the therapeutic decision making related to the assessment and diagnostic processes. The common difficulties in assessing, diagnosing, and implementing treatments with children are presented within the context of the unique qualities of childhood. The second part describes cognitive–behavioural therapy with children. The cognitive basis underlying most childhood disorders is highlighted as the rationale for applying cognitive therapy to children. This part of the book also describes some of the major developments in the area of child cognitive–behavioural therapy, highlighting a number of available techniques that can be applied to children in general and to several specific childhood disorders in particular.

The third part of the book presents a specific model for treating children based on self-control theory. This part integrates cognitive theory with developmental issues and encompasses decision making and methods for assessment, treatment, and the evaluation of the treatment's efficacy. Change and acceptance are targeted as two main forces in child therapy, with guidelines to assist therapists in selecting and adapting specific techniques appropriate to individual children's needs. Finally, this part of the book integrates the previous two parts into one systematic decision-making process for implementing cognitive therapy with children. This treatment poses a challenge to the therapist as well as to the children. The therapist must utilise both scientific knowledge and artistic creativity and flexibility. Children can benefit from the process of therapy not only by solving specific difficulties but also by gaining new skills and knowledge to control their behaviour and to grow as independent persons.

This volume is a significant contribution to child therapy. It can be read and re-read by all professionals dealing with children: psychotherapists, school psychologists, and teachers. I am delighted to have the honour of writing this Foreword.

OVERVIEW

The area of child psychology is characterised by discrepancies between its different professional disciplines and by difficulties in
integrating these disciplines into one theoretical framework for
intervention. The educational and counselling literature aims
to identify learning processes, obstacles in applying learning
methods, and difficulties in learning, attention, and concentration.
Developmental psychology is directed towards developmental issues in general, with a focus on subject areas such as children's
understanding of emotion or ability to comprehend concepts such
as time or abstract notions. Clinical psychology mainly involves
the understanding and modification of pathological disorders.
Practical theories for intervention (such as Rogerian, Adlerian, psychodynamic, behavioural, etc.) each emphasise a specific method
for changing human disorders, and some of them examine the
efficacy of the specific technique for solving the specific problem.

The treatment of children differs from that of adults in many
respects. One area of difference stems from the very nature of
childhood. Children are 'moving targets'; that is, they live within a
constant process of change. Their actions and behaviour are an
outcome of their developmental status, family processes, environmental influences, and individual characteristics. It is reasonable to
expect, then, that psychotherapy with children should integrate all
of the aforementioned factors. At the same time, therapists who
treat children need to maintain the professional expertise necessary to perform assessments, conduct the treatment process, and
evaluate its efficacy. Child therapists, in other words, must be
scientific experts in fields such as the sociology of childhood, developmental psychology, behavioural norms, and family processes, before becoming competent in the psychopathological

disorders of childhood and in the techniques and methods to treat them. Thus, in order to treat children effectively, therapists need to develop an ability to combine many pieces into one big puzzle.

Yet to integrate so many issues is not only a science but also an art. Therefore, I view child psychotherapy as both science and art. I suggest that therapists who treat children, unlike other therapists, need to be artistic—in their capacity to be flexible, creative, and interesting. Such 'artistic' attributes in a therapist can make the therapy process one that challenges the child to remain and participate fully. For many years the question has been debated as to whether people can indeed learn to be artists or whether one must be born with this gift. Today we realise that good art necessitates the combination of a scientific body of knowledge and techniques with the gifts of creativity, talent, and a propensity for art that draws the artist to his or her media.

Therapists who work well with children demonstrate an intrinsic talent that manifests itself in liking and enjoying children and in a natural affinity for understanding and creatively communicating with young minds and spirits. Yet good child therapists are those who have also mastered a range of different strategies and methods within verbal and non-verbal therapy, in order to translate successfully a variety of concepts and techniques to the child's personal level of understanding and to foster cooperation, adherence, and compliance. While an adult could say, 'Well, I don't see where my therapist is trying to go, but I heard he is good, so I'll wait and see what happens', a child will drop out if he or she does not enjoy the therapeutic process. If it becomes painful, an adult may cry but will remain; the child is likely to run away. The acquisition of knowledge and techniques must play an integral role in child therapy to enable therapists to arouse children's curiosity, interest, ambition, and challenge.

Having conceptualised child psychotherapy in general as the integration of science and art, I place an even larger and broader emphasis on this combination in specific relation to the cognitive treatment of children. Cognitive therapy with children seemingly appears to contradict children's way of thinking and ability to understand concepts, but in actuality children's characteristics merely imply the necessity of continuous adjustments, adaptations, and translations for children at different developmental stages.

During the early days of cognitive therapy—with Aaron Beck (1963) exploring the cognitive treatment of depression and with Albert Ellis (1958) centring on the treatment of neurosis—cognitive therapy accentuated the role of thoughts and emotions in behavioural change. Since that time, cognitive therapy with adults has undergone a constant process of growth, highlighting the importance of teaching clients to monitor and recognise cognitions (automatic thoughts); to recognise the connections between cognitions, affects, and behaviours; to examine the evidence for and against distorted automatic thoughts; to substitute more reality-oriented interpretations for these biased cognitions; and to learn to identify and alter the dysfunctional beliefs that predispose those experiences (Beck, Rush, Shaw, & Emery, 1979).

Although cognitive therapy has become one of the well-known and accepted scientific theories explaining human functioning, and cognitive models have become an important means for changing adult disorders, this shift has not yet characterised the area of children's psychotherapy. Cognitive therapy is still being conceived as inadequate for children due to their concrete thinking, time-limited perceptions and egocentric nature of thinking. Psychotherapy with children is primarily based on non-verbal, non-directive methods such as play or art therapy, and cognitive therapy has not become the treatment of choice for children. Rather, many therapists tend to adapt one or more specific cognitive techniques (mainly relaxation or self-talk), implementing them as part of their traditional (usually psychodynamic) treatment process.

Many books have recommended the use of cognitive techniques for child therapy in different settings. The present book differs in two main respects. First, I wish to propose one comprehensive theory for understanding children's behaviour. This theory is directed towards linking assessment to intervention and evaluation. At the same time, it focuses on applying the needed treatment via a constant process of decision making in light of the analysis of each child's individual cognitive distortions.

Second, the present book constitutes an attempt to combine several features and orientations together; namely, a developmental–educational approach will be employed to systematically apply the basic cognitive model to children, grounded in a broad cognitive

theoretical foundation and proposing a clinical intervention model
for the treatment of children. This book is founded on Beck's (1963,
1976) cognitive theory for adults as the fundamental theoretical
orientation and integrates Rosenbaum's (1990) self-control model
for adults as a specific means to apply the cognitive theory to the
domains of assessment, intervention, and evaluation. The whole
process attends to children's developmental stages and needs,
which hold crucial importance for understanding children's characteristics and for adapting suitable techniques to children's varying level of ability to follow and understand. The book, therefore,
presents cognitive developmental therapy as a treatment of choice
for children. This treatment poses a challenge to the therapist as
well as to the children. The therapist must utilise both scientific
skill and knowledge as well as artistic creativity and flexibility.
Children can benefit from the process of therapy not only by solving specific difficulties but also by gaining new skills and knowledge to control their behaviour and be independent.

Discerning child psychotherapy as a combination of clinical, developmental, and cognitive knowledge, the book comprises three
parts. The first part describes the unique features of childhood
disorders and the therapeutic decision making related to the assessment and diagnostic processes. The influences of common difficulties in assessing, diagnosing, and implementing treatments
with children are presented within the context of the unique
qualities of childhood. These complex features have been consoli-
dated into guidelines for decision making about child therapy and
about the adaptation of treatment methods to each child's specific
needs. Part I highlights the importance of the diagnostic procedure
in defining the problem at hand and in determining the need for
and type of therapy. Difficulties in assessing children are discussed
in terms of the reliability of assessors, evaluation techniques, information sources, and children's functioning in different settings.
Unique, complicating childhood characteristics are depicted, including: the normative basis for most disorders in children's development; rapid, continuous change; gaps between cognitive,
affective, behavioural, and chronological developmental stages;
and high spontaneous recovery rates. Therapist and method variables are discussed, such as the need for therapists' self-awareness
and for flexibility in child assessment and treatment methods.

Decision-making guidelines are outlined for evaluating the need for therapy in general and for adapting treatment methods to the child's particular needs, whether these methods include counselling the parents or teachers, treating the family, working with peers or in the classroom, or treating the child on an individual level. Relating to individual therapy with children, the focus is on increasing the child's motivation and cooperation in the treatment process, and on means for adapting therapeutic techniques to the child's communication level, developmental stage, skills, and abilities.

Part II of the book deliberates cognitive–behavioural therapy with children. The cognitive basis underlying most childhood disorders is highlighted as the rationale for applying cognitive therapy to children. The ability of children even at a young age to benefit from cognitive therapy is proposed, on the condition that educational and developmental features are considered. This second part of the book also describes some of the major developments in the area of child cognitive–behavioural therapy, spotlighting a number of available techniques that can be applied to children in general and to several specific childhood disorders.

Part III of the book presents a specific model for treating children based on self-control theory. This part integrates cognitive theory with developmental issues and encompasses decision making and methods for assessment, treatment, and the evaluation of the treatment's efficacy. Change and acceptance are targeted as two main forces in child therapy, with guidelines to assist therapists in selecting and adapting specific techniques appropriate to individual children's needs. Finally, this part of the book integrates the previous two parts into one systematic decision-making process for implementing cognitive therapy with children.

In the epilogue, some brief conclusions are drawn about cognitive developmental therapy and future directions for research and exploration are proposed.

Interspersed throughout the book are clinical examples and case studies taken from clinical practice. Names and some details have been changed to avoid identification of the clients.

I

DECISION MAKING IN ASSESSMENT FOR CHILD PSYCHOTHERAPY

INTRODUCTION: CHANGING THE FOCUS IN CHILD PSYCHOTHERAPY

Over the last two decades a remarkable change has occurred in society, where people have become more active participants in psychological and physiological changes relating to themselves. Social changes, new scientific knowledge, and the international explosion of the media have enabled people to have access to more information about human nature and processes. People are no longer passive concerning their own lives, but rather they wish to be an integral part of decision making relating to how they function. Individuals wish to understand why they act the way they do and to know their prognosis, and they are more involved in choosing intervention methods and processes for change.

At the same time, the development of scientific knowledge has facilitated new assessment methods and tools which result in changes in child diagnosis as well as in child psychotherapy. Yet the profusion in the area of treatment techniques, reaching a perplexing number of over 230 different methods currently in use for treating children and adolescents (Kazdin, 1988), has placed therapists in a difficult position: How can one determine the right therapy to apply? What is the 'right' therapy? How does one know what is really in the best interest of the child?

Traditional therapies emphasise the need for a lengthy, detailed, and careful assessment process, to which newly developed questionnaires, tests, and diagnostic methods are regularly added. Yet improvements in assessment methods have not changed the process of intervention itself; regardless of the length, level of detail, or outcome of the diagnostic process, traditional therapy has remained the same for the last thirty years.

During the 1980s and the 1990s a shift has characterised the area of child psychotherapy, moving from a focus mainly on assessment and diagnostic methods to a focus on outcome studies and techniques. The evolution of behavioural and cognitive techniques has fostered the achievement of rapid outcomes on the one hand (Marks, 1987; Mathews, Gelder, & Johnston, 1981; Ost, Salkovskis, & Hellstrom, 1991), together with increasing stress on valuative and comparative studies of long-term treatment efficacy on the other hand (Bergin & Garfield, 1994; Garfield, 1983; Kazdin, 1982). These phenomena have shifted the outcomes of treatment methods to the centre of attention in the literature. In contrast, the traditional emphasis on practitioners' accurate diagnostic assessment of specific problems at the time of referral seems to have been neglected. Outcome evaluation studies facilitate a clearer and more concrete definition of target problems (Sheldon, 1987), create a greater willingness to pursue goals of a modest scope (Reid, 1978; Stein & Gambrill, 1977), and contribute to the design of measures at the baseline interval and throughout the intervention process (Gambrill, 1990; Stuart & Tripodi, 1973).

However, this multitude of techniques and the aforementioned focus on comparing the effectiveness of various intervention methods, especially behavioural and cognitive techniques (Hughes, 1988, 1993), do not attend to practitioners' continual encounters with the traditional need to first assess and diagnose their clients' difficulties. Very rarely do therapists today ask themselves 'What is the best assessment or treatment method for this specific child suffering from this particular problem?' (Kazdin, 1986). Usually, each therapist consistently and regularly applies the one method in which he or she believes, to all referred children. Sheldon (1987) blames therapists for conducting 'love relationships' with their clients instead of a 'business relationship'. Those who fall in love stop asking questions and simply accept their love object as it is. Instead, a therapist, and especially a children's therapist, should conduct a business relationship with the applied methods, i.e., always continuing to ask whether yesterday's decision still applies today, whether the specific technique selected is adequate for the specific child, and if not, the kind of changes that should be made.

The tendency to highlight treatment outcomes is important. Although parents and teachers expect rapid results from the treatment of children's behaviour problems, the elimination of the presenting behaviour problem should not necessarily be the main goal of therapy. Often when the identified problem has been changed, the child continues to need therapy in order to acquire new skills (Hughes, 1993), cease avoidant behaviours (Marks, 1987), facilitate development (Kratochwill & Morris, 1993; Mash & Terdal, 1988), or change belief systems (Beck, Rush, Shaw, & Emery, 1979).

DIFFICULTIES IN OUTCOME STUDIES CONCERNING CHILDREN'S DIAGNOSES

Wenar (1982) contended that when problems occur in children, the effect can best be described as 'normal development gone awry'. Yet some children quickly show mastery, with little evidence that the challenge was other than momentary; whereas other children exhibit transient difficulties while struggling to deal with the challenge (Knell, 1993). Many researchers (e.g., Doleys, 1977) have asserted that a large proportion of problematic children will solve their problems even without intervention, considering that children are characterised by a high rate of spontaneous recovery. Others (e.g., Kazdin, 1988) have stated that only a small proportion of children in need will be referred to therapy and that referred children do not necessarily comprise that group in greatest need.

It seems that many factors may mediate children's coping with their problem, including age, gender, and individual differences. Children's therapists require a comprehensive body of research into these factors in order to contend with the myriad of difficulties and decisions confronted throughout the entire intervention process, at the stages of assessment, diagnosis, treatment, and evaluation. For example, most of the 230 different techniques for treating children that were identified by Kazdin's (1988) meta-analysis were never empirically investigated, and only a few of them were found to be effective. Very perplexing phenomena for the children's therapist are: the high frequency of behaviour disorders as opposed to the low rate of efficacy in alleviating them; and the difficulties in decision making about therapy as opposed to the potential for spontaneous recovery. However, research into problematic childhood behaviours has not yet provided a body of outcome studies that sufficiently addresses therapists' needs. Three main areas of difficulty characterise research into childhood disorders:

Difficulties in Definition

Many of the research studies relating to children make use of general definitions of problems, without offering precise definitions of the disorders (Ronen, 1993b). For example, defining a child as 'encopretic' does not take into account the different types of encopresis such as regular soiling versus soiling after long periods of constipation. The lack of accurate and specific definitions may preclude the provision of the most appropriate treatment. For instance, the intervention design for encopretic children who have developed a fear of the toilet differs from intervention methods targeting children who do not control their soiling, or from those methods needed to treat children whose soiling represents an attempt to control their parents and thus achieve secondary gains from their behaviours (Ronen, 1993c).

Difficulties in Controlling for Age Differences

Most of the outcome studies relating to children include a large range of the population, such as children between 4 and 14 years old. The 4-year-old and the 14-year-old differ qualitatively, as characterised by distinct developmental stages. For example, enuresis in a 4-year-old child may be conceived as a delay in developing control over bladder muscles or it may be considered to relate to the child's as yet small bladder, suggesting that treatment be directed towards retention control training for the elimination of enuresis. In contrast, bed-wetting in a 14-year-old adolescent cannot really be attributed to difficulties in developing bladder muscle control; therefore, enuresis would be conceived in terms of its role within the family, poor toileting habits, or low levels of self-control, responsibility, and motivation (Ronen & Abraham, 1995).

Similar age differences and developmental trends characterise most childhood disorders, such as stuttering, aggressiveness, and anxiety. For example, stuttering at the age of 4 might stem from a gap between the rapidity of specific thoughts and how quickly the child can verbalise them, whereas by the age of 6, when a child has already acquired verbal skills, stuttering is considered a problem that should be treated. Aggressiveness in a 4-year-old may reflect the child's developing ability to differentiate between himself or herself and others, as a normative step towards the development of independence; but by the age of 8 aggressiveness should be considered a deviant behaviour necessitating change. Fears and anxieties are a natural part of young children's behaviour, and children mature through overcoming fears, but by the age of 12 anxiety is no longer considered a normal behaviour.

Difficulties in Controlling for Gender Differences

Most studies on childhood disorders do not differentiate between boys and girls, although we know that boys evidence about three times more problematic disorders than do girls, excluding anxiety and anorexia (Kazdin, 1988). Gender differences may be explained by several factors, such as social norms or a variance in maturation processes. On the one hand, girls mature more quickly than boys; therefore, one can expect fewer behaviour disorders among girls. On the other hand, gender role-taking influences self-reporting, where girls tend to talk more about anxiety and fears than do boys, often resulting in higher reports of anxiety among girls (Kazdin, 1988).

Part I of this book highlights the different stages in studying and evaluating children in light of developmental and environmental issues relating to children's behaviour, in order to help the therapist make decisions about referred children during the assessment process. Although the separation of assessment from the treatment itself is arbitrary and abstract, as therapists naturally and properly integrate their client evaluations into their therapeutic undertakings, I will here embark on a separate discussion of decision making during assessment for the sake of didactic clarity. In this part of the book, some of the unique considerations involved in decision making for referred children will be discussed, and guidelines will be suggested, with one chapter devoted to each of the five conceptual stages of assessment: (1) obtaining reliable sources of information; (2) comparing the presenting problem to normative childhood behaviours; (3) evaluating whether the treatment of a child should be initiated or whether the child's problem is likely to disappear without intervention; (4) selecting the appropriate therapeutic setting; and (5) adapting and selecting appropriate treatment techniques and methods for individual child therapy.

1

OBTAINING RELIABLE SOURCES OF INFORMATION

Therapists' knowledge and understanding of different problems are frequently based on their clients' complaints and descriptions of suffering and on the personal meaning they attribute to their unwanted behaviours at the time of referral to therapy. Children, however, do not refer themselves to therapy (Kendall & Braswell, 1985). This means that, until adolescence, in order for a child to be treated, an adult (parent or teacher) must decide on the need for therapy. Naturally, the adults in charge of bringing children to therapy tend to bring those children who disturb and irritate them. Research on child referrals shows that caretakers are most concerned by children's conduct problems, referred to in the literature as 'undercontrolled behaviour' (e.g., negativism, aggressiveness, violence, disobedience). These same caretakers tend not to be aware of problems termed 'overcontrolled behaviours'—such as fears and anxieties, low self-esteem and self-confidence, and depression—which may just as seriously interfere with the child's future and development (Achenbach, 1985; Hodges, Gordon & Lennon, 1990; Mash & Terdal, 1988). These trends in adults' referrals of children determine both the kind of population that will come for therapy and the nature of the problems presented.

The process of assessment and diagnosis begins with the question: *Who can be relied on to provide accurate and relevant information about the child?* The need for systematic assessment of children is well accepted, yet significant disagreement exists regarding the questions of: which sources provide reliable information about the child?; how should childhood disorders be conceptualised?; which child characteristics, adaptation criteria, and contexts should be evaluated?; and how and by whom should assessment be conducted? (Mash & Terdal, 1988).

The three primary sources for assessment of children consist of interviewing parents or other significant adults (e.g., teachers), interviewing and testing the children, and direct observations of the children.

PARENTS AND TEACHERS AS AN INFORMATION SOURCE

Parent interviews (whether oral interviews or written questionnaires) have been considered in the past to be the major source for the assessment of children (Hughes, 1993), yet a dependence on parental information alone can lead to significant bias. Parents and children often have completely different views about their experiences, and parent–child agreement regarding the child's characteristics and behaviours has been found to be very low. Research has demonstrated that parents' perceptions of their children are influenced by their own difficulties and psychopathology (Belter, Dunn, & Jeney, 1991), their marital discord (Reid, Kavanagh, & Baldwin, 1987), and their ability to cope with their child's problem, their gender (i.e., mothers tend to be more reliable than fathers in assessing children), and the child's age (i.e., as children grow older, parents' assessment becomes less reliable) (Angold et al., 1987). These limitations question the advisability of basing assessment solely upon parental interviews, implying the need to take into consideration any knowledge available regarding the parents themselves in order to determine the reliability of the information they provide.

Teacher interviews (again whether oral or written) may serve as another source of information from significant adults in the child's environment. In addition to providing information on academic difficulties, teachers can be very important for reports on children's social adjustment (e.g., observing the child's behaviour within the peer group or disobedience in the classroom), as well as on general behaviours such as hyperactivity. However, similar problems arise with regard to the reliability of teacher reports and their correlation with those of parents and of the children themselves. Research has shown that teachers, like parents, tend to accentuate children's disruptive behaviours, whereas they tend to underestimate internalising problems such as anxiety, fears, and depression (Hodges et al., 1990).

THE CHILD AS AN INFORMATION SOURCE

The second assessment source consists of interviews, self-report questionnaires, and formal diagnostic testing of children. A collection of tools for formally assessing children's behaviour has been promoted in the literature, such as intelligence tests, achievement scales, instruments tracing developmental level, projective evaluations, and behaviour-based measures (Gelfand & Hartman, 1984). Structured questionnaires have been shown to be more reliable, but they have limitations due to their basis on the child's ability to read, write, and understand written texts or due to the child's different cultural or socio-economic level which may influence the outcomes. On the other hand, projective tests avoid the need for reading and writing skills but are significantly more subject to the tester's personal interpretations, as related to the tester's cultural and socio-economic level and interpretation of the raw material. Usually a battery of several diagnostic tests is utilised. A battery may include, for example, the Bender Gestalt Visual Motor Test, the Wechsler Intelligence Test for children (WPPSI or WISC-R), the Human Figure Drawing test or a similar variant, and two projective personality tests—the Rorschach inkblot test and the Children's (or Thematic) Apperception Test (McMahon & Peters, 1985; Ronen, 1994a). Such a battery attempts to account for the disadvantages of the different assessment instruments and to facilitate the validation of test results through more than one indication of each finding. However, it should be remembered that children's performance during testing is related not only to the instruments and to the children's skills and abilities, but also to their motivation, relationship with the diagnostician, and the timing and setting of the test. Any testing procedure first and foremost requires the establishment of a good rapport with the child.

A verbal interview with the child in the assessment process—where he or she describes the referred problem and the thoughts and feelings it elicits, interprets its meaning, and is given an opportunity to express wishes for its resolution—is a crucial source of information on the child's perceptions of self (e.g., self-esteem, emotions) and the environment. Children's self-reports of acting-in behaviours (i.e., overcontrolled or internalising behaviours such as depression and anxieties) have been found to be more reliable than parental reports in this domain (Achenbach, 1993; Kazdin, 1988). On the other hand, children's self-reports of acting-out behaviours (i.e., undercontrolled or externalising behaviours such as disruptiveness and oppositional defiant disorders) have been found to be less reliable than parental reports of such conduct.

These findings are not surprising in light of the fact that acting-out behaviours are manifested more overtly in the environment, and are more easily recognised and appraised by parents than are emotions and self-images. In addition, undercontrolled children tend to attribute their problems to the environment, not to themselves, evidencing an external locus of control that diminishes the reliability of their self-reporting. It is important to view children's self-reports not as valid truths representing an objective reality (i.e., 'the child is depressed') but rather as the child's own perspective on inner feelings and behaviour (i.e., 'the child feels depressed' or 'the child sees herself as suffering from depression'). Moreover, self-reporting may be influenced by a number of situational variables (e.g., the child's mood, hunger, fatigue; the presence of the parents), by the tester–child relationship, and by the type of self-evaluation (e.g., retrospective versus immediate). Yule (1990), for example, demonstrated that post-traumatic children often do not disclose information in the presence of their parents, for fear of upsetting the parents with their true negative feelings.

As a result of the differences between parent–teacher reports and child self-reports, Achenbach (1985) suggested five sources of information: parental evaluations, teacher evaluations, cognitive evaluation of the child, physical condition, and clinical evaluation. He claimed that the combination of these five sources allows for the standardisation of the child's assessment.

DIRECT OBSERVATION AS AN INFORMATION SOURCE

The third source for assessing children—direct observation—helps the therapist to become acquainted with the child and his or her behaviour within the child's natural environment. Direct observations reduce the dependency on parents' memories or subjective interpretations and on other misleading factors (Hartman & Wood, 1982). However, direct observation necessitates obtaining permission from the family, nursery, kindergarten, or school environment being observed, and also involves the investment of time and energy to work with the environment in preparation for the observer's visit. The goals and procedures for the observation must be planned in order to remain as non-intrusive as possible in the home or classroom and to attain the desired information. Usage of the direct observation method forces the therapist to invest the time and effort into visiting several of the child's natural environments and/or conducting several observations in each setting. Proponents of the observation method claim that the child's natural behaviour differs in his or her various environmental settings, rendering only one observation in one setting insufficient. Although the clinician tends to trust observational data that have been directly obtained, these data require validation due to the possible impact of the observer's presence in the setting; the paucity of research on the merit of various structured observation techniques; and the questionable reliability of non-structured methods that necessitate personal interpretation and judgement on the part of the assessor (Gelfand & Hartman, 1984).

The following case example from my clinical practice accentuates the importance of weighing the reliability of information sources:

A mother asked to meet with me before I met with her son. She was a single mother of a 12-year-old boy whom she had been raising alone since he was aged 2. She expressed concern about her son who had been diagnosed as having learning difficulties and who now, two weeks prior to beginning intermediate school, was overanxious. She described a child who avoided social activities and was starting to develop social loneliness. The mother was also concerned about her son being a 'parental child', caring about her too much. A teacher's report pointed to the fact that the child, although exhibiting learning difficulties, coped wonderfully in a regular classroom. The teacher described him as a child who was able to interact with peers but usually preferred to be friends with 2–3 other children and hated large crowds. She mentioned that he always played with children during school recess and that he was chosen by others to participate with them in different activities. Meeting with the child impressed me with a handsome boy, full of charm, who made fun of his mother's worries: 'She's too nervous, and she makes a mountain out of every molehill.' He simply stated: 'Yes, I told a friend of mine that I don't want to go to the new school, but who wants to start school? Any normal kid would rather continue vacation! Sure I'll go to school. Why does she even listen to my conversations with my friends?' This example indicated that some children referred by significant adults in their lives do not need therapy. In this case the boy did not require help either with preparing for the new school or with his social activities, but the mother did need guidance in letting go of her son and toning down her worries.

GUIDELINES FOR THERAPISTS ON ASSESSMENT STAGE 1: THE SOURCE OF DIAGNOSTIC INFORMATION

Based on the strengths of each source of information, the following guidelines may be helpful:

- Parental reports should be utilised to disclose the child's acting-out behaviours (i.e., disobedience, aggressiveness, negativism, hyperactivity, impulsiveness).
- Teacher reports can provide excellent information on the child's assessment in relation to age norms (e.g., academic functioning, social interactions with peers and adults outside the family, communication style).
- Children's self-reports are the best window into understanding thinking style and emotions (e.g., self-esteem, self-concept, anxiety, depression, loneliness).
- Direct observations should be employed when the previous sources of information contradict each other or when there is a need for more accurate baseline information.

- Having collected information from the various sources, try to assess whether the different sources of information coincide into one whole picture or whether one contradicts the other. Conflictual outcomes should be further examined.

SUMMARY

Reports that a given child has problems does not necessarily indicate that the child needs therapy. Also, evidencing problems in one setting does not always correlate with deviant behaviour in another setting. Therefore, an important step in assessment consists of collecting reliable information relating to the child's functioning in different settings (with family, school, and peers) and relating to the child's own perceptions of the specific problem.

2

EVALUATING PRESENTING PROBLEMS IN TERMS OF NORMATIVE CHILDHOOD BEHAVIOURS

In order to make diagnostic decisions, the assessment process next continues by asking, *What is normal behaviour and what is deviant?* Epidemiological studies and large-scale surveys of young children suggest that behaviour problems are quite common in pre-schoolers. Unlike in adults, most maladaptation experienced by children (e.g., fears, anxieties, enuresis, encopresis, conduct disorders, social deficits) initially appears as normal developmentally related behaviour. This normative basis for common childhood phenomena hinders the differentiation between a normal developmental reaction and a behavioural dysfunction. Age criteria are usually relied upon to determine when a behaviour previously considered normal becomes maladaptive; however, the cut-off ages are equivocal.

Recent epidemiological studies found that 17–22% of youngsters under 18 years old in the United States have emotional and behavioural problems (Kazdin, 1994). A classic review of the most frequent problems referred by mothers to a children's clinic (Lapouse & Monk, 1958) revealed the overlap between developmentally appropriate and inappropriate behaviours:

—*Fears and worries* (43% of referrals) are a normal and necessary part of children's development. Research has shown that young children normally experience between four to seven fears (Barrios & Hartman, 1988; Kratochwill & Morris, 1991). A 2-year-old's intense fear of dogs would be considered natural but a similar fear would be viewed as an anxiety disorder in need of treatment at the age of 10 (Wolman, 1982).

—*Bed-wetting* (17% of referrals) is expected for children under 4 years of age. Yet, no consensus exists regarding the age to intervene with therapy. At the age of 3 or 4, children who wet their beds do not need therapy but rather the parents may be referred to counselling with regard to toilet training practices that do not give children's unwanted behaviour unnecessary attention. Bed-wetting at 6 or 7 years of age is usually considered to be an unwanted behaviour in need of treatment.

—*Thumb or finger sucking* (10% of referrals) is a normal habit among infants and is seen as a clear problem among adolescents, but the childhood years are debatable regarding the need for treatment. This problem also seems to recover spontaneously and is not generally reported among adults, raising the question of the need for intervention despite the relatively high rate of referrals.

—*Stuttering* (4% of referrals) is a normal phenomenon at around 4 years of age, when a gap emerges between the child's pace of thinking and of talking, as the child starts developing whole ideas for discussion. Continued stuttering at the age of 6 may be considered a reason to turn for help (Kessler, 1966).

Many children demonstrate problem behaviours at some point in time, although few will exhibit such behaviours to the extent that they are considered indicative of serious psychopathology (Campbell, 1990). The brief review above highlights the importance of age as a central consideration in the decision of whether or not to treat a child with a specific problem.

DIFFICULTIES STEMMING FROM CHILDREN'S CONTINUOUS CHANGE AND SPONTANEOUS RECOVERY

Children constantly and rapidly change as they grow up (Kratoch-will & Morris, 1993; Schaffer, 1990), frequently complicating the diagnostic and assessment process. Very often what seems to be a problem at one point in time spontaneously disappears without any intervention. Levitt (1963) found an approximate 73% improvement rate among children who did not receive treatment. These spontaneous changes complicate decisions about treatment. Many times when parents enter therapy for their children, they suddenly claim that the original problem reported during the assessment period has already been resolved but that another problem has risen in its stead. Therefore, in order to reach a decision regarding the need for treatment, the therapist should make a prediction based not only on general knowledge regarding spontaneous recovery for this specific difficulty area, but also on the pace and development of the specific child's problem up to the present time: What is the probability of the problem disappearing? Will it remain stable, improve, or become worse?

DIFFICULTIES RELATED TO THE GAP BETWEEN CHRONOLOGICAL, COGNITIVE, AFFECTIVE, AND BEHAVIOURAL STAGES OF DEVELOPMENT

Determining expected 'normal' behaviour for a certain child is often difficult due to a discrepancy prevalent between his or her chronological age and his or her emotional, cognitive, and behavioural age (Sahler & McAnarney, 1981). Such gaps, which often characterise children, create a challenge for the therapist who is attempting to assess and diagnose an individual child referred to therapy.

The following example illustrates the need to have familiarity with children's normal behaviour at different ages and stages of functioning in order to execute the assessment process appropriately.

An 8-year-old child was brought to therapy because his parents thought he acted overly childish. Without relating to the child's different levels of functioning, the therapist could easily have suggested that he be trained in the skills he lacked. However, careful assessment revealed that the boy's cognitive level was more characteristic of a 10-year-old child. In view of his high intelligence, it seemed that the child's environment related to him as older than his chronological age, thus he was also expected to act emotionally like a boy two years his senior. When he could not meet these expectations, his parents thought him to be childish, but in fact his behaviour was age-appropriate. Decision making for this young boy's difficulties concluded that the parents, rather than the child himself, required intervention. The parents were instructed in how to relate to their son and in what to expect from him.

DIFFICULTIES IN EVALUATING CHILDREN'S DIFFERENTIAL FUNCTIONING ACCORDING TO ENVIRONMENT

In view of children's strong dependence on their environment, prominent diagnostic tools for assessing children rely on parents' and teachers' evaluations. In the previous chapter, the problems stemming from a dependence on significant adults for information on the child were described, underscoring research that demonstrated a significant incongruence between different figures' evaluations of the same child's behaviour (Kendall & Braswell, 1985). Another major difficulty arising from assessments based on the child's environment is the child's responsiveness to different settings. A child can evidence disruptive behaviour only at home or in one specific classroom—for example, if she dislikes the subject or feels uncomfortable with the teacher. These disparities make it difficult to determine whether the child has specific deficits or whether he or she has been conditioned by an environment that gives positive reinforcement to certain unwanted behaviours. Such a differentiation is crucial within a comprehensive assessment process, fostering the decision of whether the child or the wider environment should be the target of intervention.

DIFFICULTIES RELATED TO CHILDREN'S PERSONAL LANGUAGE AND INDIVIDUAL THINKING STYLE

The individual styles, habits, attitudes, and language of children can pose a challenge for therapists during the assessment process. A variety of methods available to children's practitioners exists not only with regard to treatment methods but also in diagnostic assessment techniques for evaluating children's problems. The large majority of non-verbal, unmediated therapeutic modes such as painting, free association, and story-telling depends on each therapist's interpretation of the child's responses. Although the reliability or validity of these interpretations cannot be substantiated, the need to conduct a deeper inquiry into the child's personal attributions and thinking processes should be maintained as an important principle during assessment. Standard testing procedures, unfortunately, rarely incorporate the children's own explanations regarding their specific responses to test questions.

Awareness of idiosyncrasies in language and age-appropriate difficulties in communication should always be maintained during child assessment procedures. Two cases described to me by the central probation office in Israel illustrate this point. In these investigations, children's testimony was considered unreliable in court, while in fact the problem was related to understanding the children's language.

> One very young girl who was questioned about the place where she had been raped insisted it was 'on the closet'. The judge after many questions decided she was not telling the truth. The social worker, after the hearing, had the opportunity to take her aside and asked her to point to 'on a closet'; the girl pointed to the top of a table.

> In another court case, a boy said that he had been abused about a year earlier, but at a later inquiry he said it had been during the winter (only two months before). Only a knowledge of children's developmental limitations in their concept of time could help differentiate between the possibility that this child evidenced a difficulty in time perception or in the understanding of concepts and the possibility that the child was lying.

The following brief case descriptions exemplify the problems inherent in evaluating children without carefully examining the children's own explanations for their behaviour:

> A 12-year-old boy was referred to my private clinic by his school psychologist. She was worried that something was wrong with this child, who painted 'crazy things'. When asked to paint a picture of his family, the boy instead had painted the laundry machine, the dishwasher, and the oven. The psychologist was concerned about the child's painting of objects instead of people. A discussion with the boy revealed that on the day of the drawing he felt very critical and angry with his mother for always working around the house, and he blamed his entire family for doing nothing but cooking, baking, and cleaning over the weekend, thus depriving him of a two-day family trip he had wished to take.

In another case:

> A 9-year-old daughter of divorced parents was referred to me by her mother, with whom she lived. The mother was very anxious because, during recent months, the girl talked incessantly about death and murder, which aroused her mother's fear that her daughter might commit suicide. During the second assessment session, the girl revealed that her father had not come to visit her for the past six months, and that he was a policeman serving in a homicide department. She herself explained that her interest in death and dying was her way of expressing her wish to see her father. She was afraid to express this wish directly to her mother because of the mother's negative response whenever the father was mentioned.

Another example:

> A girl painted her family with all their sex organs visible. Her teacher was afraid that the girl was trying to report being sexually abused. Careful investigation clarified that, one day earlier, the mother had bought the girl a book on sexual education and taught her about human anatomy. Naturally, the next day's painting reflected the new learning.

The following case demonstrates the additional importance of familiarity with children's individual areas of interest and hobbies, in order to achieve effective assessment.

A university student practitioner receiving psychodynamic supervision requested my consultation on a series of paintings by a 12-year-old child in his treatment. The child's drawings were very strange—full of snakes and robot-like human figures. Without knowing the child, it was very easy to interpret the snakes as sexually symbolic and the robots as representing a problem the child had with his internalised parental figures. However, a familiarity with the boy's hobbies facilitated the recognition of the robots and Ninga turtles featured in the boy's favourite video films. The therapist's awareness of contextual factors enabled him to consider alternative hypotheses for the repetitive themes in the child's drawings, such as a desire for strength, an outlet for aggressive impulses, an attempt to acquire peer approval through mastering drawings of popular characters, etc.

GUIDELINES FOR THERAPISTS ON ASSESSMENT STAGE 2: WEIGHING THE REFERRED BEHAVIOURS IN COMPARISON TO THE NORMAL BASE OF CHILDHOOD BEHAVIOUR

The following questions should serve as guidelines:

- Does the presented problem have a normal developmental explanation?
- Does the behaviour change or is it constant?
- Could it be a result of inconsistencies in the child's chronological, cognitive, emotional, and behavioural ages?
- Does the child function similarly in different environments?
- Could the behaviour be a result of the child's linguistic or thinking style, attitudes, or routines?

SUMMARY

This chapter suggests that it is impossible to treat children without a careful grasp of the unique features characterising childhood. Assessment of child behaviour should include developmental considerations, an interest in issues related to diagnosis and classification, an ongoing evaluation process, a concern for prevention, and an emphasis on environmental influences on the child (Mash & Terdal, 1988). Schaffer (1990, p. 21) suggested that:

> A view [of childhood] will need to be modified from time to time as new findings are uncovered but which is not dependent on any one specific study or set of studies and instead reflects the general thrust of knowledge currently available about children's development.

3

DECISION MAKING ON THE NEED FOR THERAPY

The therapist's process of decision making during assessment entails successive stages of continually asking questions. This chapter will address the question *Does this child need therapy or not?*, which must be raised before attempting to decide *What is the right setting for treatment?* (see Chapter 4). All of these questions require careful consideration in view of research demonstrating that traditional forms of child therapy (i.e., painting, playing) showed no better improvement rates than did spontaneous recovery (Kazdin, 1988).

The decision to initiate therapy can easily be made in extreme cases where the child is at serious risk (e.g., an abused child, a case of anorexia nervosa, a child who has attempted to commit suicide, etc.) or when the environment is experiencing severe distress (e.g., in cases of disruptive behaviour, aggressiveness, violence, etc.). When distinct risk situations are not the case, the decision of whether treatment of the child is necessary becomes more difficult.

Therapists, who are immersed in the world of mental health and obviously reveal an openness to the idea of sharing problems and receiving help for difficulties, sometimes lose sight of the fact that the general population continues to attach stigma to psychotherapy (Schaffer, 1990). The negative impact of entering therapy due to a fear of stigma (e.g., embarrassment if friends find out), fears of therapy (e.g., anxiety about the therapist's 'magical' or mind-reading powers), and the concurrent effects on self-esteem (e.g., a sense of failure or shame) should not be ignored. Good therapists will address these emotional reactions at the onset of establishing the therapeutic relationship. However, if, for example, the gain to be achieved in therapy is expected to be mild, or the rate of spontaneous recovery is high, we therapists should learn to turn prospective clients away in their best interests. Furthermore, the effect of being assessed by a professional and then told that one's (or one's child's) problems are 'normal' (or at least do not necessitate treatment) cannot be underestimated as a motivating factor in the subsequent processes of coping with and overcoming those very problems.

To address the necessity for therapy, a number of factors should be examined, including the comparison of the presented behaviour with diagnostic criteria and with environmental and age norms; the stability of the problem; future risk if untreated; the behaviour's known responsiveness to treatment; and the child's motivation level.

COMPARISON TO DIAGNOSTIC REFERENCES

Assessing children's deviant behaviours requires a comparison with recognised diagnostic criteria. The most widely used diagnostic manual, the *Diagnostic and Statistical Manual of Mental Disorders* (DSM-IV, American Psychiatric Association, 1994), defines disorders; utilises indices based on the duration of the problem, severity of impairment, and number of dysfunctional behaviours; and provides information on associated features and predisposing factors.

COMPARISON TO ENVIRONMENTAL NORMS

Another means towards child assessment consists of evaluating whether the child's peers behave similarly. For example, if most of a young girl's peers avoid staying alone at night, she might not be demonstrating fears and anxiety but rather may be modelling the patterns of behaviour of others in her environment. On the other hand, if most of a boy's classmates began reading by the age of 7, yet he, already 10 years old, still cannot read, he can be considered deviant from his environmental norms and should be evaluated to uncover what is preventing him from behaving like other children of his age.

COMPARISON TO AGE NORMS

Children's presenting behaviours should also be assessed to determine if they are appropriate to age norms. For example, a 10-year-old child deviates from age norms when exhibiting fears that are typical for a 5-year-old. A 5-year-old may be considered to be acting inappropriately for her age when she is distressed by such problems as the family's economic situation, which usually do not affect children before adolescence.

STABILITY

Questions concerning the stability of problem behaviours should be addressed not only through the use of a reliable diagnostic reference manual but also through careful collection of historical data from the family and, if necessary, school. The stability of behaviour should serve as a guideline for determining whether or not a referred child needs therapy. Many problems that appear in diagnostic manuals are transitory and modifiable among children. For example, a child can develop a tic following surgery, but recovery will usually occur spontaneously within several days or weeks. Only if the frequency of the problem remains stable should therapy be considered. Similarly, if an unwanted behaviour increases in frequency or severity, this can provide sufficient reason to initiate therapy, even when a problem is brief in duration or does not seem to endanger the child's future. For example, a child who began to wet her bed following a car accident might be expected to stop bed-wetting no more than 3–4 weeks later. However, if the frequency of bed-wetting incidents increases from two to five times a week, the child should be referred to treatment.

FUTURE RISK

An important consideration when determining the need for therapy consists of evaluating the extent of risk to which the child will be exposed in the future if the disorder is not treated. Sometimes the nature of the problem is such that there might be a long-lasting effect on the child's future. For instance:

> A child who was a good student but started failing examinations upon entering junior high school should be considered a potential candidate for treatment. In this case, although there is reason to believe that the youngster with a strong academic history will be able to overcome these failures and improve his/her grades, it is recommended that the student receive help in identifying the source of the new problems (e.g., test anxiety, poor learning habits, lack of motivation, pre-adolescent fears and anxieties, or other sources of emotional disorders) in order to prevent the accumulation of failures and frustrating experiences that may have a negative impact on self-esteem and confidence.

PROGNOSTIC INDICATIONS

Due to the fact that childhood problems are not intrinsically pathological and are exhibited to some extent by most children, available knowledge should be tapped concerning the known responsiveness of the child's specific problem to various treatment modes. Decisions regarding whether or not to treat often depend on prognostic implications (Achenbach, 1985). Two projections should be developed regarding: (a) whether the behaviours are likely to remain the same, improve, or deteriorate in the absence of treatment, and (b) whether that outcome will differ as a function of differing treatments.

An important factor in this stage of assessment is to determine the extent to which the problem has affected the child's personal, academic, social, and emotional functioning. For example, if parents of a 5-year-old bring their child for evaluation because of thumb sucking, drinking from a bottle, or continued use of a pacifier, a sharp distinction can be made between two types of referrals. Child A has been significantly affected by his problem: he is immature socially and linguistically for his age; his oral activity has precluded him from talking or playing with other children because he prefers sucking to using his mouth or hands for other exercises. In contrast, the effect of the problem on Child B has been insignificant: at home he enjoys sucking the bottle, thumb, or pacifier, but his functioning in all other areas is appropriate, and he even drinks from a cup outside the home. We might refer Child B to a dentist, but from a mental health perspective, the treatment will not precipitate emotional growth. Therapy for Child A, however, would be indicated in order to facilitate significant emotional maturation.

As described above, therapists expect that some behaviour problems will not cause harm to the child's future and that some will be outgrown by the child. Yet even when a good prognosis for spontaneous recovery is indicated, therapy may still be recommended when the literature demonstrates a high probability for eliminating the referred problem (e.g., thumb sucking, nail biting, tics). In instances where research and clinical experience have led to less conclusive findings, the child's motivation can be a key factor in making the decision of whether or not to treat.

MOTIVATION

The justification for treatment sometimes lies not in the problem itself but rather in how the child and his or her environment cope with the problem. At times the prognosis for a referred problem is not very promising and the problem does not appear to pose a risk for the child's future, but the child and his or her parents and/or teachers have great motivation for change. This set of factors constitutes a positive indication for treating the child, despite the probability that change may occur very slowly and require much effort. For example:

A 12-year-old child had overcome stuttering through therapy. He stopped therapy a year previously, when he could already speak fluently and his stutter was barely noticeable. At this stage, only people who knew about the boy's previous difficulty were sensitive to the slight fluctuation in the fluency of his speech, which occurred when he was nervous. Six months later the boy asked to return to therapy in order to deal with the minute remainder of his stuttering problem. It seemed that an enormous amount of effort would be necessary to overcome this small but persistent deficiency, but its major importance for the child and his parents offered sufficient indication to continue therapy.

GUIDELINES FOR THERAPISTS ON ASSESSMENT STAGE 3: DOES THE CHILD NEED THERAPY?

The following table (Table 1) can enhance decision making about the child's need for therapy. It should be remembered that none of these factors is independent; their combination is important.

Table 1: Criteria for referred behaviours: determining the need for treatment

Behaviour	Need for therapy
Resembles diagnostic criteria	Yes
Suits environmental norms	No
Suits the child's age	No
Has improved	No
Is stable or has worsened	Yes
Risks the future	Yes
Has a good prognosis	Yes
Sparks strong motivation for change	Yes
Is important to child and family	Yes
Has changed an existing situation	Yes
Is conducive to spontaneous recovery	No

SUMMARY

Many times when a child is referred to therapy, and the child as well as the parents agree to cooperate, therapy will be applied no matter what the problem is. This chapter suggests that therapy is not something to be habitually prescribed in response to parental or other initiative. Rather, a very careful assessment should be carried out in order to obtain sufficient answers to a set of questions relating to the need for therapy, including: comparison of the referred problem to developmental features (whether the behaviour suits environmental norms or age norms); data from clinical diagnosis (diagnostic criteria, stability of the problem, risk for the future, good prognosis, a significant effect on the child); familial considerations (importance for the family, motivation for improvement); and personal variables (motivation for change, the potential to facilitate significant change). The results of these analyses should assist therapists to make the decision as to whether therapy is needed or not. Therapists must learn to ask themselves the question: Is therapy recommended or could the child function better without it?

4

DECISION MAKING ON THE THERAPEUTIC SETTING

After making the decision that a given child does need therapy, the next stage in the assessment process constitutes the selection of the most appropriate setting for treatment. The criteria for selecting the optimal setting should be related to the therapeutic aim, the 'cause' of the presented problem, and the child's developmental stage.

THERAPEUTIC AIMS

The treatment of children often involves preventative targets that have implications for selecting the treatment setting. These therapeutic aims comprise one of three possible objectives:

—*Primary prevention:* Therapy is directed towards preventing future problems among children.
—*Secondary prevention:* Therapy is directed towards treating a problem that already exists, with a focus on preventing its generalisation to other areas.
—*Tertiary prevention:* Therapy is directed towards decreasing existing problems that pose a risk to the child's future.

When the therapeutic aim is primary prevention, the usual solution will be not therapy but rather an educational intervention (e.g., counselling and guidance) in the environment. Such primary-prevention level interventions would include working with at-risk children in groups (e.g., preparing children for the transition to first grade) or conducting parent-training groups (e.g., among parents of adolescents).

When secondary prevention is the major therapeutic aim, it is usually recommended to treat the child within his or her natural environment, including guidance or counselling to the system itself (i.e., teachers, peers, parents, or family as a whole). The treatment focuses on the interaction between the individual and the system, and on improving communication and negotiation skills in particular. For example:

> Secondary prevention is a concern for the child who is disruptive in class, when the child does not exhibit a conduct disorder or aggressiveness but rather can be disciplined, is a good student, and has a positive interaction with the teacher. This child's difficulty lies in his yelling out the answers, calling out of turn, and interrupting other pupils; his behaviour is disruptive to the class and disrespectful to his peers, creating resentment from his classmates and frustration from his teacher. However, it emerges that, because the child generally knows the correct answers, the teacher has reinforced this negative behaviour by listening to his outbursts. Treatment would focus on the interaction between the child and the teacher, on ways to encourage the child's development of self-control and restraint, and on means for the teacher to reinforce appropriate behaviours.

Tertiary prevention as a therapeutic aim is activated when a problem already exists necessitating direct treatment. Even if the environment did in fact play a role in its development, the problem usually will not improve without directly treating the child, whether through individual or group therapy.

THE 'CAUSE' OF THE PROBLEM

Identification of the 'cause' of the problem can also enhance decision making regarding setting selection. The three 'causes' for a child's problem can be described as when the child is (a) the cause of the problem; (b) a victim of the problem; and (c) a part of the problem. Children may need direct treatment when they are either the cause or the victim; when they are merely a part of the problem, environmental treatment is usually most appropriate.

These distinctions can be illustrated by an example of each type. The child who is the *cause* of the problem would be, for instance, a child with learning disabilities who has self-esteem difficulties, or a child with aggressiveness or anorexia. The second type, for example, would be a child who has been abused, who is not the cause of the problem but is rather its *outcome*. Children are often referred to therapy due to problems for which they are not responsible, but which are an outcome of environmental processes. Nonetheless, children who are victims of their problems typically need help (e.g., dealing with trauma and guilt feelings) as do their parents. The third type is familiar to therapists from referrals where the child is the 'identified patient', but the intake process reveals that he or she is only *part* of the problem. Even when the child is labelled as the cause of the problem being referred, this does not necessarily mean that the child should be the direct recipient of treatment. Cases such as disobedience problems are often related to the child's interaction with parents or teachers and are sometimes even a reflection of marital discord; therefore, appropriate school, family, or marital therapy should be considered.

DEVELOPMENTAL STAGE

Forehand and Weirson (1993) suggested that the therapeutic setting should be designed to account for developmental factors. The child develops different roles at each childhood stage, requiring a specific treatment plan best suited to facilitate the new roles. The main developmental role of infancy comprises the shift from total dependence on the mother figure to a first step towards independence. It follows that problems in gaining initial achievements in autonomy at this stage should be met with therapy in the form of parental counselling. The main role of early childhood consists of developing skills in academic domains and social situations; therefore, therapy should involve parents, teachers, and friends and should be directed towards educational-therapeutic assignments.

The main roles to be developed in middle childhood to adolescence entail self-identification and self-control, indicating that therapy at this stage should be directed towards the child through individual treatment.

Young children usually do not receive direct therapy before the age of 5 years; however, if the child has the verbal and cognitive abilities and motivation for treatment, he or she can be considered a candidate for individual therapy from 4 or 5 years. From 4 to 7 years, it is preferable to have the child present, regardless of the setting, and to have the child involved even if the parents are the focus of therapy. Child therapy at this age most likely centres on gaining cooperation or support, facilitating developmental processes, and enabling a positive experience. As a general rule, therapists tend to treat children individually only from the age of 7.

SETTING CHARACTERISATIONS

An adult referred to therapy usually receives individual therapy and sometimes marital or family counselling. A child's therapy offers many more settings from which to choose: parents' counselling either as individuals or in groups; counselling the child's school environment (teachers, school counsellor); treating the child within the natural setting (e.g., with peers, in the classroom, or through family therapy); or treating the child directly through individual or small group therapy.

It would be emphasised, however, that because the cognitive–behavioural approach underscores the relationship between the person and the environment, and because the child's natural environment is the family, whenever a child is concerned, the family will be involved in treatment—even if the problem is in school. When I discuss the decisions about setting, I am referring to the decision of whom to term the client(s). Yet at some level the parents will always be involved—whether to facilitate the child's cooperation, to support the child's therapy or the school intervention, to receive counselling themselves, or to be an integral part of a family treatment.

TEACHING, COUNSELLING, AND SUPERVISING THE ENVIRONMENT

In general, when a child is young or the problem is related to normal development or to educational or nurturing problems, treating the child's environment should generally be considered the treatment of choice. Defining the environment as the direct client is appropriate when the child does not seem to manifest an independent problem but rather evidences a difficulty that appears related to his or her relationship with the environment. This may be appropriate for children ranging in age from birth through adolescence (Ronen, 1993a). The methods focus on teaching and supervising the child's environment rather than the child (e.g., parent groups, parent counselling, teacher counselling, working with the school counsellor), with the goal of facilitating adults in the environment to become agents of change. The therapist's areas of required specialisation regarding this setting include: normal child development (e.g., developmental stages, expected age-appropriate norms), common problems among children (e.g., difficulties in sleeping, eating, learning), behaviour change techniques (e.g., reinforcement, punishment), communication skills, supervision skills (e.g., ability to train and supervise others), and treatment techniques such as modelling, role playing, leading discussions, videotaping, and developing and using manuals (Ronen, 1993a).

Interventions with the environment aim to help parents and educators to understand children better, to acquire skills for changing behaviour, and to increase their effectiveness in educating children and improving child discipline. The intervention goals consist of enhancing the significant adults' knowledge about normal development, eliciting the sharing of experiences, and supervising the adults in implementing effective methods for behavioural change, such as reinforcement, punishment, and avoidance techniques. A review of the research (see Ronan, 1993a) has pinpointed the ability of parents and teachers to change childhood disorders effectively by changing themselves and the consequences of the child's behaviours.

TREATING THE CHILD IN THE NATURAL ENVIRONMENT

This second intervention setting focuses on a specific problem needing treatment (i.e., secondary prevention), in contrast to the former method that is often directed towards general counselling and supervision (i.e., primary prevention). When the child's disorder is deviant but related to interactions with peers or family, or when the problems are connected to communication styles, roles, and patterns, it is recommended that the child be treated within his or her natural environment. This setting is selected for one of two reasons: (1) the child is the identified client but the problem stems from a systemic difficulty (e.g., in relationships, communication style, secrets, coalitions); or (2) the child's behaviour problem is being reinforced or sustained by the environment (family or peers) and cannot be treated without changing the environment's attitude or behaviour towards the child. Families and peers whose behaviour is maladaptive for an individual within the system or for the whole system constitute the target population in this setting. Usually, the individual child is of elementary to high school age and will show signs of emotional or social distress.

This group of methods focuses on the treatment needs of the child's environment, whether that implies the implementation of family therapy, classroom training procedures, or a peer group intervention. The intervention goals consist of helping the system identify how its members communicate with and influence one another, and teaching the system new communication skills and how to apply them more satisfactorily. The specialisation areas required for the therapist applying treatment of the child within the environment include: systemic approaches, group processes, techniques for leading groups, social and communication skills, and techniques such as discussions, role playing, modelling, rehearsal and practice.

INDIVIDUAL OR SMALL GROUP THERAP
CHILDREN

In line with tertiary therapeutic aims, direct treatment of the child is usually conducted after eliminating all of the other aforementioned possibilities (i.e., parent counselling, family therapy, educational counselling, working with classmates or peers, etc.). Two options for direct treatment with children are available: individual or small group therapy.

Small group therapy is based on the existence of a group whose members all share a common problem. Group therapy is specifically indicated when the child's problems are related to social dysfunction, where the group sessions serve as opportunities to identify social deficits and to learn and practise new interpersonal skills. For other problems, sharing within the group setting offers youngsters the potential to identify with other children and thereby reduce their sense of loneliness or of being different, enhancing self-esteem. A crucial aspect of group therapy is the receipt of support through peer interaction, especially useful in problems of addiction, anorexia, etc. Group therapy is often applied concurrently with the individual therapy, to strengthen specific domains of need.

Several presenting problems should be considered during the assessment process as a clear indication for individual treatment of the child:

—When the child presents a disorder that should be decreased, or when its main cause necessitates further careful identification (Kazdin, 1988).
—When the child lacks specific skills or demonstrates poor self-esteem, self-evaluation, or social skills (Mash & Terdal, 1988).
—When the child presents a high frequency of behaviours (e.g., aggressiveness) that should be decreased because of their disruptive effect on the environment (Kazdin, 1987).
—When the child presents an avoidant behaviour that interferes with normal functioning (Marks, 1987).
—When the child continues to present disruptive behaviour after the environment has been changed (Ronen, 1993a).
—When the child poses a risk to himself or herself or others.

—When the child demonstrates self-destructive behaviours that place him or her at risk (Sheldon, 1987).

Individual therapy is usually not applied before 7 years of age (or entrance into elementary school) and is employed up through adolescence. The intervention's goals consist of: improving children's functioning, increasing adaptive behaviour, imparting self-control, and desisting with deviant behaviour. The areas of specialisation required for therapists include: child psychopathologies, children's disorders, specialised techniques for treating children, group processes, techniques for leading groups, and treatment techniques such as discussions, role playing, modelling, videotaping, painting, using games, stories, and music.

Important considerations regarding available treatment settings are illustrated in Table 2 including the type of intervention facilitated by each setting.

CASE EXAMPLES

The therapist's ability to make an optimal decision on treatment setting can be difficult even when the child evidences a major problem for which clear research findings are available as to the efficacy of the therapist's preferred techniques (Ronen, 1993a). However, most often, the child referred to treatment exhibits multiple problems, complicating the decision-making process even further. In the following case of multiple symptoms, the treatment setting recommended to help solve one problem may not necessarily suit another.

A girl aged 10 was referred to me for therapy, with the main complaint of primary nocturnal enuresis. A careful interview process revealed several other behaviours with different histories: low school achievements from the time she entered school, very limited peer relationships beginning three years earlier (following a move to a new environment), and tics that started only one month prior to referral (following the girl's one-week hospitalisation) (Ronen, 1993a). On the basis of research on treatment outcomes, the initial evaluation of this girl indicated the following treatments of choice: (a) the bell and pad method for her enuresis

Table 2: Treatment setting characteristics

Setting	Type of intervention	Child's age	Presenting problems	Aims
Parent group	Educational	All ages, especially young	Normal development	Providing information, support
Individual parental counselling	Educational, therapeutic	All ages, especially very young, adolescents	Behaviour problems, disobedience	Imparting skills for change
Teacher counselling	Educational	School age	Under-controlled	Imparting skills
Class intervention	Educational	School age	Social	Modifying norms, interactions
Family therapy	Therapeutic	School age	Communication	Modifying communication, roles
Group therapy	Therapeutic	Pre- to late adolescence	Any disorder	Changing behaviours, imparting skills
Individual therapy	Therapeutic	Kindergarten and up	Any disorder	Changing behaviours, thoughts, and emotions

(Doleys, 1977), required individual therapy and parent counselling; (b) the competition response model to quickly eliminate tics (Azrin & Nunn, 1974), necessitating only individual therapy; and (c) social skills training using group practice for her social problems (Cartledge & Milburn, 1986), suggesting the need for group therapy. The low school achievement would necessitate further evaluation in order to determine whether the problem derived from a low intellectual level, inappropriate learning habits, learning difficulties, lack of motivation, anxiety, etc.

The following case exemplifies the importance of careful assessment for the right decision about the therapeutic setting.

> The client was a 15-year-old boy referred by his parents to therapy. The parents described their son as having 'gotten off the right track', by listening to heavy rock music, dressing in black, making drawings of skeletons and weapons, going out with friends to pubs, and returning home late at night. The decision-making process (Assessment Stage 2) pointed to the fact that this boy's behaviour did not deviate either from his age group or from the norms characterising his environment. He was not behaving differently than were most of his friends. Continued assessment stressed the fact that, although his behaviour was deviant according to his parents' expectations, the boy was a good student; the youngsters with whom he socialised were also considered 'good' children; and the so-called deviant behaviour did not harm the environment or his functioning in school. On the other hand, the parents were new immigrants in the country, and this was their oldest child. While he adjusted quickly to the new neighbourhood, they did not, and they expected him to study all the time, listen to 'good classical music' and dress like 'a proper human being'. Some form of intervention was deemed necessary due to the frequent family arguments and quarrels, including the son's angrily running out of the house. The decision regarding treatment setting was narrowed down to two alternatives: counselling the parents to help them in accepting new social norms and behaviours and in accepting their child as is, or family therapy to work on trying to change the communication style within the family. There seemed to be no indication for individual therapy with the boy.

GUIDELINES FOR THERAPISTS ON ASSESSMENT STAGE 4: SELECTING THE OPTIMAL SETTING FOR TREATMENT

The following questions can facilitate therapists' decision making:

- Could the referred problem result from the parents' lack of knowledge about normal development?
- Could the problem result from the parents' inability to foster the child's obedience?

- Could the problem be a reflection of poor communication styles, roles, and patterns within the family?
- Could the problem be related to deficiencies in the teacher's discipline methods?
- Could the problem be a result of peer interactions or social skills?
- Could the problem be a reflection of the child's thoughts, beliefs, and emotions?

SUMMARY

In the previous chapter, I proposed that it is not obvious that where there is a problem there is a need for treatment; in this chapter, I emphasise the fact that when a child presents a deviant behaviour, this does not imply that the child needs to be changed; rather, it means that questions should be raised about who is the source of the problem, who is responsible for the current situation, who can be changed, and what kind of change could best help all of the members of the family.

Preventative therapeutic aims and the child's developmental stage must be taken into consideration. When it is possible to work with the family or the parents (or, alternatively, the teacher and school counsellor), there may be no need to treat the child directly. The home or school may be counselled or may be involved in interventions targeting the child within his or her natural environment. The decision to treat a child directly should be taken only when such treatment is assumed to be the most effective way to help the child function.

5

INDIVIDUAL THERAPY WITH CHILDREN: ADAPTING TREATMENT TECHNIQUES AND METHODS

After deciding whether the presenting problem is a normal developmental behaviour or is deviant and whether it necessitates intervention, the individual treatment setting has been selected. However, making the decision that a given child's problem necessitates individual therapy is not the end of the assessment process but rather a good starting point for designing the treatment. Determining that the child needs individual therapy leads to another decision-making process presented in this chapter: *How do I mobilise the child to cooperate?* and *What kind of strategies and techniques best suit this child?* Answering these questions will help place the therapist in a good position to understand the specific child and the best way to treat the presented problem, leading us to the second and third parts of this book where cognitive therapy is applied to children of different ages and with various problems.

CREATING THE MOTIVATIONAL ENVIRONMENT FOR INDIVIDUAL THERAPY

A critically important and often difficult task in child psychotherapy lies in the creation and maintenance of the necessary therapeutic environment. Children come to therapy because they have
been brought, but they will not remain in therapy unless they like
the therapist and enjoy the therapeutic process (Ronen, 1993b). The
quality of the relationship constitutes one of the most important
features in individual child therapy (Brandell, 1992). Children will
not continue treatment if they are bored, cannot easily express
themselves, or if the therapist does not succeed in stimulating their
curiosity, motivation, and participation (Kazdin, 1988; Ronen,
1992). The therapist must utilise play activities, create a climate of
trust, and establish a meaningful affective relationship with the
child (Rose & Edelson, 1987). The choice of techniques is determined by a variety of factors including the child's interests, preferences, and developmental stage and the limitations in the
therapist's technical repertoire (Brandell, 1992; Ronen, 1992).

ADAPTING TECHNIQUES TO THE CHILD'S COMMUNICATION LEVEL AND STYLE

Therapists need to be keenly aware of the child's language in order
to use it for communication in therapy. This includes tuning in to
the child's specific interests and day-to-day experiences in order to
provide content areas, familiar to the child, that will serve as a base
of reference in therapeutic communication with the child. To increase the child's enthusiastic involvement, drawing, playing, or
talking may be employed. These communicational requirements
imply that therapists must participate actively in the child's natural
environment, become familiar with the important figures in the
child's life, and be flexible in the use of different methods for
helping the child.

ADAPTING TECHNIQUES TO THE CHILD'S DEVELOPMENTAL STAGE

Decision making during the assessment process, regarding the kind of treatment technique to be selected in individual therapy, should address the child's developmental stage (Ronen, 1995). A critical issue related to young children in therapy is that of their cognitive functioning. Being aware of the child's cognitive level, strengths, and limitations enables the therapist to design the cognitive process and techniques in a way that will appropriately meet the child's developmental needs (Knell, 1993).

Piaget's work (1926) classified children's cognitive development into four stages, including three that have implications for individual therapy:

—*Sensorimotor stage* (birth to 2 years): Children have limited cognitive and language skills and explore their environment predominantly through sensory and motoric means. Therapy is directed towards the child's environment.

—*Pre-operational stage* (2 to 7 years): Children evidence rapid conceptual and language development, and thinking becomes symbolic. The child could be a good candidate for individual therapy as long as the therapist remembers to use symbolic language and appeal to the child's illogical way of thinking and dealing with concrete concepts. 'Experiential' therapy, using painting, art, music, dancing, etc., could best fit the child's ability to learn.

—*Concrete operational stage* (7 to 12 years): Children's thinking remains concrete and egocentric, yet abstract concepts can be understood in a limited way, and rapid academic learning occurs. Verbal therapy can now easily be applied, if based on the child's day-to-day life and experiences, not on universal concepts, notions, and rational arguments.

—*Abstract (formal operation) stage* (from age 12): In pre-adolescence and adolescence, children develop an adult-like way of thinking, including dealing with abstract and holistic concepts. Verbal therapy can now be seen as an interesting challenge; whereas non-verbal therapy may even be insulting to the young person who wishes to be treated like an adult.

The child's cognitive developmental sophistication must be considered in designing intervention strategies (Bierman & Furman, 1984; Knell, 1993). A good match between the developmental level of the child and the level of complexity of the selected intervention is critical. In designing the proper strategies, the therapist should therefore ask: *What does a child at this stage need?* If the child is in a stage where experiential learning is the most meaningful, then play therapy could best fit the child's needs. Where language and verbal skills are already acquired, as in pre-adolescence, play therapy might be viewed as childish. Verbal therapy at this stage may best facilitate the child's eagerness to use new linguistic abilities for describing experiences and emotions. In general, age, cognitive functioning, and the nature of the presenting problem all have an impact on selecting a verbal versus a non-verbal therapeutic mode—as can be seen in Table 3, which illustrates the common criteria for selection.

MATCHING THEORIES AND TECHNIQUES TO CHILDREN'S NEEDS AND THERAPISTS' INCLINATIONS

In this fifth and final stage of assessment, two main decisions should be taken:

Table 3: Criteria for selecting the therapeutic mode for individual child therapy

Variable	Non-verbal therapy	Verbal therapy
Age	Young children, up to 7 years	Middle childhood, from age 7 up to adulthood
Cognitive skill level	Less advanced	Higher skills
Kind of problem	Internalising, overcontrolled	Externalising, undercontrolled

Source: Ronen (1995). © 1995 Springer Publishing Company, Inc., New York 10012. Used by permission.

1. Which is the one theory that suits this individual child with his or her specific problem and that I, as a therapist, believe in and can apply?
2. What kind of technique(s) could best help me achieve my aims?

As a cognitive–behavioural therapist, who envisions therapy as a scientific process of problem solving and who emphasises the empirical measurement of outcomes, I myself consistently address the first question with the same answer. I view behavioural and cognitive therapies not as techniques but as a way of life, as a theoretical approach and as a way of looking at one's behaviour and trying to change it. With regard to the second decision, professionals tend to confuse theory-based approaches (whether behavioural, psychodynamic, Adlerian, etc.) with the various methods or techniques used to accomplish them, such as verbal, play, or art therapy. Hence, behaviour and cognitive therapies with children are often conceived as direct, verbal interventions, while psychodynamic therapy with children is usually conceived as indirect, non-verbal therapy. Instead of these overgeneralisations, a strong need exists to differentiate between theory and techniques. Just as psychodynamic therapy can be verbal even with children, it is possible to conduct cognitive and behavioural therapy both directly and indirectly.

As an illustration, if a boy exhibits low self-esteem, in psychodynamic therapy he will usually be treated through play therapy, letting him express his feelings of inferiority, shyness, and lack of self-confidence through play or painting and then through the acceptance of the therapist. In the therapeutic setting which creates such an accepting atmosphere, the boy will develop self-acceptance and follow it with an improvement in self-concept and self-assurance. Behaviour and cognitive therapy with such a child, on the other hand, could be conducted both in verbal and non-verbal terms. I could treat the boy verbally, teaching him to change his way of talking to himself, and the way he thinks and acts. For example, he can be shown how every time he wants to invite a friend over he tells himself: 'She probably won't want to come over. She'll just pretend she's busy', thus leading the boy to negative feelings and to an avoidance of calling the friend. Or, I could use play therapy in a cognitive–behavioural orientation (Knell,

Table 4: The four alternatives in child cognitive–behavioural therapy

	Direct	Indirect
Verbal	Direct talk or discussion about events, behaviours, and feelings	Reflective communication (talk about others, such as in bibliotherapy)
Non-verbal	Direct use of play, art; being a model for change	Use of art and play without directly relating to it

1993), where I serve as a model for positive self-talk. I can try to modify the child's paintings by proposing darker colours, heavier lines, and bigger figures for him to draw. As the boy learns to change the paint, his sense of coherence will also be changed. In sum, with such a child, cognitive–behavioural therapy allows me to conduct either direct therapy (by directly changing or modifying the child's behaviour through verbal training) or indirect therapy (by using art techniques for a change).

In general, cognitive–behavioural therapy can provide four alternative treatment techniques, as shown in Table 4.

As can be seen from Table 4, it is possible to apply direct verbal therapy (talking with the child about the problem, trying to change the way the child functions through modification of thoughts and behaviours) or direct non-verbal therapy (using art to demonstrate to the child different alternatives for behaving). Therapy can be indirect verbal treatment (talking about what other children would do in the same situation) or indirect non-verbal treatment (using stories to exemplify the wanted behaviours or using art and play without directly intervening, enabling the child to understand for himself or herself how to relate these to the problem).

CASE EXAMPLE OF THE FIVE ASSESSMENT STAGES

The following example will demonstrate the five stages of assessment for making decisions about a child's therapy.

An 8-year-old girl, 'Maya', was referred to therapy by her parents who were worried when they found out that their daughter had been sexually abused by a 13-year-old male neighbour. The parents reported that their daughter was suffering from a major trauma that might endanger her future development. *Assessment Stage 1* (examining the sources of information and trying to match the parental reports with those of the daughter) revealed that Maya was anxious but not traumatised. The boy did not physically hurt her, and while having the relationship with him she felt it was pleasant for her. The boy made her touch him and took off her clothes. She liked the boy and enjoyed being with him and having his attention, but after three months she began to feel she was doing something wrong and might be punished. She then developed tics, sleep disturbances, and a fear of separation, but all those behaviours related more to her fear of her parents' response than from the sexual episodes.

Assessment Stage 2 revealed that her problematic behaviours were deviant for her age, environment, and developmental stage and were the outcome of her premature sexual experience rather than a normal behaviour. *Assessment Stage 3* (determining the need for therapy) pointed to the fact that Maya's experiences had changed her own as well as the family's functioning, creating tension and pressure in all their lives, indicating the need for treatment.

For *Assessment Stage 4* (deciding who should be treated), the parents were assessed as having handled their daughter appropriately. They had been able to reinforce her for telling them the truth about her sexual encounters and offered support and understanding; on the other hand, they were also able to clarify to her that this was inappropriate behaviour at her age, and that she was not ready for sexual relations without developing anger, guilt feelings, or shame. They offered her therapy in order to help her understand why this was not the time for her to continue a sexual relationship and to help her cope with the experience so that she would not develop a post-traumatic disorder. It seemed, therefore, that the parents did not need counselling (other than letting them know that Maya was not at risk), indicating individual therapy as the treatment of choice.

Assessment Stage 5, the final stage of decision making, concerned techniques for individually treating the child. Maya was very shy and had difficulty—even avoided—talking about recent events and problems. On the other hand, she was very creative and enjoyed art and especially sculpturing, suggesting that art therapy sessions might be a much quicker and easier means to gain her cooperation. Therefore, an indirect therapeutic method (art therapy, using sculpturing and painting) was selected, applying a cognitive approach with clear goals and a structured process of change aimed towards changing her beliefs, thoughts, and emotions.

GUIDELINES FOR THERAPISTS ON ASSESSMENT STAGE 5: SELECTING THE TECHNIQUES TO APPLY

Four questions should guide the therapist in assessing which techniques to apply in individual child therapy:

- Does the child's developmental stage enable verbal therapy?
- Does the child have the ability to sit still, listen, and concentrate?
- Does the child have motivation for therapy, or should play therapy be implemented to establish motivation?
- Does the child have verbal skills, or is he or she better in art, music, dance, or play?

SUMMARY

The separation of assessment from therapy is artificial but necessary for purposes of clarification. Therapy actually begins when first meeting a family, during the first intake session. The therapist's initial interview style, comments, and questions already effect changes in the family's functioning. As such, the assessment process itself often helps family members to better understand their problems and even to solve them. When the problem is not solved during the assessment stages, the selection and adaptation of the most beneficial technique for the specific client is the last formal decision necessary before starting the treatment process. I view these first five stages of assessment as a time for consulting, appraising, clarifying, and checking my perceptions and evaluations before initiating therapeutic work aimed directly towards the specific goal of treatment.

II

DEVELOPING COGNITIVE THERAPY WITH CHILDREN

INTRODUCTION: THE ULTIMATE QUESTIONS

The traditional approach to child therapy has focused on play therapy based on a psychodynamic orientation. In their paper reviewing issues in child therapy, Kendall and Morris (1991) emphasised the fact that the field of therapy with young people has evolved dramatically over the last half century. A view of psychodynamic therapy as the only acceptable psychotherapeutic approach to children has evolved into an acceptance of family therapy and behavioural therapy as two common forms of child psychotherapy. Still, there are precious few controlled studies available to determine which specific form of treatment is best suited to each specific type of disorder among children and adolescents. The need to adapt the treatment type to the individual child's characteristics and type of problem has re-awakened the traditional 'ultimate questions' for therapists (Paul, 1967): What treatment, by whom, is most effective for this individual, with this specific problem, in this set of circumstances?

In a way, this question represents a regression to old areas of professional interest, after many years when therapists and researchers have invested their major efforts into improving assessment tools and therapeutic methods. Nevertheless, regression is a necessary part of childhood development, and the treatment of children stimulates the need to adapt our means to the child's nature. Therefore, it is not surprising that we as therapists follow such regressive tendencies by returning to an old, traditional way of thinking about our work, namely the 'ultimate questions'. In childhood development, a unique pattern presents itself—that of the U curve—where forward movement towards a new stage is followed by a temporary regression to previous functioning. For example, children who are learning to walk regress frequently to the crawling skills they had previously mastered. Children who have already learned to talk clearly and loudly, and to add two or three words together, begin stuttering and get 'stuck' as they develop the ability to combine ideas into a whole story. Parents often complain about their children who had been able to stay alone in the dark but suddenly began exhibiting a fear again. Children who already have self-confidence, social skills, and an ability for self-control often demonstrate signs of regression as they move from kindergarten to school, developing separation anxiety, increasing their rate of anxiety in general, and regressing in social skills and self-control (Shein, Ronen & Israelshvilly, 1995).

Temporary regression is a natural tendency within development, as children move from one stage of development to the next. A good metaphor would be that of a car that stalls before reaching the crest of a hill; in order to climb over the top, the driver must regress, reversing a little bit, and then push the gas down harder to try to overcome the obstacle.

Advancement in child therapy has many benefits: better assessment tools, more efficient intervention methods, and greater knowledge of human disorders that enables specification. Yet advancement holds risks and deficiencies. Trying to specialise in disorders may move attention towards the problem, diverting the focus away from the person and the treatment process. Definitions, questionnaires, and treatment manuals help to make the process of therapy shorter and more efficient, but may also lead many therapists to feel that they 'know the answer' before even knowing the client, or to adapt preconceived solutions to a general idea about a problem instead of seeking out the individual person behind the problem. Perhaps these pitfalls we all face in our attempts towards progress in the field of psychotherapy should remind us of the simple truth and relevance of old, traditional ideas such as Paul's ultimate questions.

If we look carefully at these questions, they are divided into three domains: the client, the problem, and the therapist or therapeutic features. Part I of this book was devoted to the first domain—the child as a client—focusing on the unique characteristics of childhood and natural developmental trends in order to trace their influence on the assessment (and, later, on the treatment and evaluation of the therapeutic process). Part II of the book discusses the second and third domains. First, the cognitive nature of childhood problems will be addressed, based on the characteristics of problematic children and how they affect treatment. Second, the nature of therapy will be examined, highlighting techniques and strategies in cognitive therapy. Part III will combine these sections into a practical guide for the therapist in the complicated but challenging application of cognitive therapy with children.

In this part of the book I focus on the basic deficits and distortions which characterise disturbed children, proposing that the most frequent behaviour problems typifying children are those resulting from cognitive disturbances. Different types of problematic childhood behaviours are linked to their cognitive basis, and the clear cognitive changes depicting children during their development are described, emphasising that the solutions to childhood problems should also be based on cognitive features and, therefore, that children are natural candidates for cognitive therapy.

Chapter 6 focuses on the cognitive elements underlying childhood behaviour problems, relating to cognitive distortions and deficits. 'Good' therapy is conceptualised as meeting the cognitive needs of the child and his or her problems. Obstacles in therapy are also considered: the rate of dropout, regression, and difficulties in generalisation. Chapter 7 presents the basics of cognitive therapy, highlighting its roots in behavioural therapy. In Chapter 8, I describe how cognitive therapy can be effective if adapted appropriately to children's developmental needs and abilities. Chapter 9 presents and illustrates techniques and strategies available for child cognitive therapy. Finally, Chapter 10 provides case examples for applying cognitive techniques to several predominant childhood disorders encountered by therapists, delineating the ways in which cognitive therapy has been applied to children over the last two decades.

6

THE LINK BETWEEN COGNITIVE THERAPY AND CHILDHOOD BEHAVIOUR PROBLEMS

This chapter presents cognitive elements underlying childhood behaviour problems and proposes cognitive therapy as a solution for the described disorders.

CHILDREN'S COMMON BEHAVIOUR PROBLEMS AS CORRELATED WITH COGNITIVE FEATURES

As described in Chapter 2, behaviour problems occur very frequently among children and might be viewed as a natural, integral part of childhood. In fact, children to a large extent may be regarded as growing up and maturing through coping with these very behaviour problems and trying to eliminate them, live with them, or decrease their frequency.

Epidemiological studies of children have identified the following behaviour problems to be the most frequent (from most to least common): temper loss, overactivity, fears and worries, restlessness, sleep disorders, enuresis, food intake, nail biting, tics, and stuttering (Lapouse & Monk, 1958). Table 5 presents the prevalence, sex ratio, and family incidence of common behaviour disorders according to the DSM-IV (American Psychiatric Association, 1994). A careful look at these behaviour problems

Table 5:   Diagnostic criteria for the most frequently referred behaviours

Problem (DSM-IV number)	Prevalence	Sex ratio (boys : girls)	Family incidence
Separation disorder (309.21)	Very common	Equal	More frequent in children of mothers with panic disorder
Overanxious disorder (300.02)	Very common	Equal	More frequent with mothers having overanxious disorder
Oppositional defiant disorder (313.81)	Common	More common in males	No information
Conduct disorder, aggression (312.8)	11%	9 : 2	More common in families with antisocial personality disorders
Enuresis (307.6)	10%	3 : 1	75% have at least one parent who was enuretic
Tics (307.21)	5–24%	3 : 1	No information
Stuttering (307.0)	5%	3 : 1	Strong familial incidence
Nightmare disorder (307.47)	5%	3 : 1	Strong familial incidence
Sleep terror disorder (307.46)	1–4%	More common in males	Common among first-degree relatives
Attention-deficit/hyperactivity disorder (314.01)	3%	6–9 : 1	Over-represented

points to some shared features: their high frequency of occurrence in the overall population with no relation to cultural or social background; their higher frequency among boys than girls; and the familial link highlighting the fact that most children with these disorders have at least one parent who evidenced the same disorders as a child (Ronen, 1992). All three of these features can be accounted for by cognitive explication.

The findings for childhood disorders regarding spontaneous recovery, gender ratio, and family incidence can all be related to deficiencies in cognitive skills, and particularly to one component within the framework of cognitive deficits: a lack of self-control. As children acquire self-control they are expected to become better able to overcome difficulties, postpone gratifications, and control their behaviour. The natural increase in cognitive skills such as self-control during development may be related to children's spontaneous recovery without therapeutic intervention. With regard to gender, the finding that most of the common childhood difficulties are more prevalent among boys than among girls may also be related to the higher ability for self-control found among females. The majority of aforementioned childhood problems run in the family, facilitating the conceptualisation of the familial incidence level as related to self-control theory (Ronen, 1992). Studies in the area of cognitive therapy in general, and of self-control skills in particular, have shown the link between a lack of self-control and the existence of behaviour problems.

Many therapists recognise the importance of the child's cognitive representation of events and experiences in the development of common childhood problems such as phobias, conduct disorders, and learning difficulties (Powell & Oei, 1991). Cognitive therapists relate these childhood disorders to a general deficit in cognitive skills. Kazdin (1988) noted that children with deviant behaviour suffer from deficiencies in particular processes or from an inability to use or apply cognitive skills. For example, conduct disorders in general and antisocial disorders in particular are viewed by cognitive therapists as undercontrolled behaviour patterns characterised by a lack of problem-solving skills (Kendall, Reber, McLeer, Epps, & Ronan, 1990), poor generalisation skills, deficits in social reasoning, and misinterpretations of social situations (Akhtar & Bradley, 1991). An investigation of the role of cognition in anxiety disorders has led to the proposal that anxious children present more negative self-evaluations, negative self-speech, and more off-task thoughts (Kendall, 1994). Social cognitions have been found to affect the social adjustment of children, specifically in terms of deficits in global cognitive constructs such as perspective taking, role taking, and referential communication (Crick & Dodge, 1994). Depression has also been linked to cognitive elements (Baron & Peixoto, 1991), whether in the form of deficits in active information processing as can be seen in hyperactivity (Kendall, Stark, & Adam, 1990) or in terms of self-control skills, attributional style, self-esteem, helplessness, and hopelessness (Kaslow, Rhem, Pollack, & Siegal, 1988).

Children exhibiting behaviour problems such as hyperactivity, impulsivity, and aggression can be differentiated (Ronen, 1992) from children who do not have behaviour problems with regard to their tendency to:

1. Generate fewer alternative solutions to interpersonal problems.
2. Focus on ends or goals rather than on the intermediate steps towards obtaining them.
3. See fewer consequences associated with their behaviour.
4. Fail to recognise the reasons for other people's behaviour.
5. Be less sensitive to interpersonal conflict.
6. Be unable to predict their own behaviour.
7. Be unable to evaluate and reinforce their behaviour.

In sum, as presented above, childhood disorders have been directly connected to cognitive deficits or distortions. Therefore, cognitive therapy seems to be a natural treatment solution.

COGNITIVE THERAPY AS A SOLUTION TO OBSTACLES IN CHILDREN'S THERAPEUTIC PROCESSES

No matter what kind of therapy is applied with children, a high rate of success is usually shown—perhaps due to the transient nature of childhood disorders. Still, together with the high success rate, children's therapy is characterised by a high rate of dropout, a significant extent of regression, and difficulties in generalisation.

Dropping out of therapy can be related to child, parent, or therapist characteristics. The fact that children do not refer themselves to therapy, but rather are referred by parents or teachers, highlights one possible source of dropout. While the referring adult may have one view of the child's difficulties, needs, and wishes, believing that the child needs therapy, the child may perceive himself or herself very differently, objecting to the treatment process, resisting cooperation, and eventually desisting.

Dropping out can also occur due to an incongruence between the expectations, aims, or wishes of the therapist and of the parents. For example, parents may expect rapid change while the therapist aims for slow, gradual change (Kazdin, 1988). Or parents may emphasise one problem (such as a disruptive 'acting-out' disorder), whereas the therapist is more concerned about an 'acting-in' disorder such as anxiety or depression. The therapist's difficulties in adapting his or her way of thinking to the child's tempo, language, and areas of interest could also contribute to dropout.

Regression to behaviour problems that improved during treatment may be related to the transient nature of childhood disorders, to the rapid changes in therapy, or to the termination of the therapeutic process at the time when change is achieved, instead of continuing therapy until a period of consistent, steady changes has been maintained (Ronen & Wozner, 1995; Ronen, Wozner, & Rahav, 1992). Overlearning methods have been suggested as strategies for eliminating regression (Doleys, 1977). Controlled studies that compared cognitive therapy to other methods for treating childhood disorders have suggested that the main benefit of cognitive therapy for children lies not in the rate of success but rather in the fact that the rates of dropout and regression have been found to be much lower than in other methods (Ronen & Wozner, 1995; Ronen et al., 1992).

Studies carried out in recent decades have shown a large gap between outcomes at the termination of therapy and at a follow-up interval (Kazdin, 1988), pinpointing the limited success in generalising the outcomes outside the therapeutic setting. A major goal in intervention consists of achieving a consistent behaviour change in appropriate situations external to the intervention context (i.e., transference of the effect from the intervention setting to the home, school, or peer group) (Morris & Kratochwill, 1991; Rose & Edelson, 1988). Generalisation is especially relevant with children, who undergo a constant process of change and face many challenges while attempting to overcome common childhood difficulties.

Yet, despite its importance as a therapeutic aim, generalisation has been shown to be especially problematic with children (Baer, 1985). Different effects have been revealed by outcome studies on children, according to factors such as the location of the study (i.e., an intervention setting or the natural setting such as school or home), the point in time at which assessment was completed (i.e., immediately after the intervention's termination or after a follow-up period) (Ronen et al., 1992), and the behaviours investigated (i.e., the behaviour that had been treated or other, similar, behaviours) (Kazdin, 1988).

Behavioural, like cognitive, theories are interested in applying the needed skills in order to solve behaviour problems. Behavioural models consistently apply specific skills to specific disorders in order to decrease undesired behaviours. However, these models often limit the change to a specific treatment goal, setting, or behaviour, restricting the child's ability to generalise achievements and to generate new skills and behaviours based on changes accomplished in therapy. Cognitive therapy, on the other hand, resembles the application of learning methods (e.g., reading, writing, analysing a poem) in that it is directed towards applying more general skills that will enable the child to independently self-solve new problems in the future, by using learned cognitive skills and by being able to generalise them in other difficulties and settings.

Generalisation, therefore, comprises the founding rule in cognitive therapy for children. Gresham (1981) suggested that generalisation should receive as much attention as initial skill acquisition. It has been suggested that, in order to facilitate the occurrence of generalisation, steps should be taken to introduce the necessary mediating behaviours into the child's repertoire and to provide encouragement for a wide range of generalisable situations. Therapists can integrate generalisation into the intervention regimen, and a plan should be established early in intervention for maintaining progress and generalising skills beyond the boundaries of time and place. Initially, the focus of intervention should be placed on developing the intervention plan, but as immediate change is obtained, greater emphasis should be placed on planning for generalisation (Rose & Edelson, 1987; Ronen, 1994b).

Several authors have outlined intervention guidelines for increasing the likelihood of generalised improvement. Meichenbaum, Bream, and Cohen (1985) utilised multiple trials in different settings and tasks; anticipation of potential as well as real failures and their coordination into the intervention programme; and a performance-based rather than time-based termination of training. Robin (1985) suggested the use of solutions, additional discussions or debates to be held at home, and tasks incorporating newly acquired skills or attitudes into daily living. Rose and Edelson (1988) differentiated between strategies for the generalisation of actions that occur within the intervention setting (e.g., increasing responsibilities, varying examples, preparing for setbacks, conceptualising specific experiences) and of actions that take place primarily in the child's natural environment (e.g., working with parents, teachers, and peers; training beyond termination).

Research has demonstrated that cognitive methods have lower regression rates and produce a stronger generalisation effect than do other methods such as pharmacological, non-verbal, and purely behavioural treatments. A meta-analysis of 108 controlled studies investigating treatments with children showed more favourable outcomes for behavioural and cognitive techniques than for non-behavioural techniques (Casey & Berman, 1985; Weisz, Weiss, Alicke, & Klotz, 1987).

GUIDELINES FOR THERAPISTS: LINKING COGNITIONS TO CHILDREN'S DISORDERS

Based on the description of cognitive elements underlying childhood disorders, and the proposed cognitive therapy as a solution, the following guidelines may be helpful:

- Examine the cognitive features accompanying the problem that could represent a combination of the child's developmental status and the behaviour problem. Which deficiencies or distortions can you identify?

- Can you identify some of the deficiencies that were presented in this chapter as characteristic of the referred child?
- Carefully examine the child's motivation and cooperation and the parents' expectations. How can you prevent dropping out? What overlearning plan can you devise to prevent regression? How should you work towards generalisation?

SUMMARY

Cognitive theory views childhood disorders as resulting from deficiencies or distortions in the child's cognitive skills, therefore directing therapy towards imparting the lacking skills to children. Based on this assumption, cognitive theory addresses the main obstacles characterising childhood therapy: the high frequency of success versus the high frequency of dropout and regression. Cognitive therapy focuses not only on the elimination or solving of problems but also on preventative targets and the ability for generalisation.

7

THE ROOTS AND DEVELOPMENT OF COGNITIVE THERAPY WITH CHILDREN

This chapter will present behavioural elements that have influenced the development of cognitive therapy with children.

THE BEHAVIOURAL ROOTS OF CHILD COGNITIVE THERAPY

Cognitive therapy with children is an extension of the fundamental behavioural therapy which was traditionally based on systematic applications—from modern learning theory to the treatment of psychiatric disorders, using classical, operant, and modelling learning (Eysenck, 1959). More recent behavioural treatments have utilised concepts and strategies representing a prototype-based view of behaviour therapy (Mash & Terdal, 1988), which emphasises the importance of an empirical basis but not of children's developmental needs. According to these researchers, behaviour therapy is devised empirically, based on the results of behavioural assessment (Gelfand & Hartman, 1984). The role of contemporaneous determinants of behaviour, rather than early life events, is accentuated (Hughes, 1993), and treatment efficacy is evaluated on the basis of changes in observable behaviours (Gelfand & Hartman, 1984). Work in the field of behaviour therapy focuses on the need to adapt different treatments through the use of multivariate statistical methods such as factor analysis and cluster analysis (Achenbach, 1985) and on the use of written manuals, videotapes, and documentation for repeated treatment outcomes.

Many of the cognitive techniques that are used to treat children and adults are the same as those used in behavioural therapy. For example, social skills training is now considered a cognitive strategy but has very deep roots in behaviour therapy, using models, rehearsal, and role plays. Similarly, relaxation is an important technique in cognitive therapy, but Jacobson (1938) developed it and Wolpe (1982) used it as part of desensitisation in classical behaviour therapy. Exposure therapy was developed by Isaac Marks (1969, 1978, 1987) as part of operant conditioning, but in cognitive therapy it was amended to focus on self-exposure as a necessary skill in overcoming difficulties (especially for learning to accept emotions; Rosenbaum, in press). Redefinition, as a mode of changing cognitive translations and as part of cognitive restructuring, has deep roots in behavioural therapy, where it was used to enhance clients' positive thinking and empowerment. If we continue to look at each and every technique, we can see that in a different way each has been applied before.

Behavioural therapists did not develop specific techniques for children, but rather adapted techniques and knowledge from the adult world to meet the specific needs of the child. The techniques share some common behavioural methods through which the content of treatment is delivered, such as modelling, role playing, and behavioural contingencies (Kendall & Braswell, 1982).

The most popular techniques for children are those derived from operant and modelling learning as they are applied to externalising disorders such as aggressiveness. Applications of the operant method have included: use of contingency management based on positive and negative reinforcement (Hersen & Van Hasselt, 1987; Ronen, 1991); overcorrection (Lovaas, 1967); behavioural contracts (Vaal, 1973); and extinction and punishment as well as token economy (Hughes, 1993). These techniques, regularly used by adults while training children, are clear, concrete, and can easily be followed and understood by the child.

Children are naturally exposed to techniques based on modelling as part of their maturation process even without their awareness (Bandura, 1969, 1977), for example, in sex roles, social skills, social interactions, etc. Using modelling in therapy is usually accompanied by other techniques such as self-talk or reinforcement. Positive outcomes have been shown for the use of modelling with children in: teaching how to cope with anxiety (Bandura, 1969; King, Hamilton, & Ollendick, 1988; O'Connor, 1972); instilling social skills (Bornstein, Bellack, & Hersen, 1977); teaching how to deal with stress (Meichenbaum, 1979, 1985); and helping to learn to stop and think before acting (Kendall & Braswell, 1982).

Techniques based on classical conditioning, such as relaxation and desensitisation (Wolpe, 1982) are more difficult to administer to children. These methods necessitate special adaptation through imagery, self-instruction, reshaping of procedures, brevity of instructions, parental help, games, paint, play, candies, and toys that may increase the child's motivation and ability to relax (Koeppen, 1974; Morris & Kratochwill, 1983; Ollendick & Cerny, 1981). Promising results using classical techniques have been reported for the treatment of internalising disorders such as school phobia (Lazarus, 1960; Taylor, 1972), noise phobia (Tasto, 1969), toilet phobia (Jackson & King, 1981), and separation anxiety (Montenegro, 1968). However, the lack of controlled studies relating to internalising disorders does not permit definitive conclusions regarding the efficacy of classical behavioural techniques for children.

Specific cognitive-mediation techniques for children based on behavioural theory include, but are not limited to, self-instruction training, self-management strategies, problem-solving training, attribution retraining, and relaxation training (Magg & Kotlash, 1994). Children who have been taught to use cognitive-mediational strategies to guide their behaviour have been shown to improve their adjustment (Durlak, Fuhrman, & Lampman, 1991).

As described above, cognitive therapy with children has its roots in behavioural therapy, but it has also been widely influenced by cognitive therapy with adults.

BASICS IN COGNITIVE THERAPY

Cognitive therapy is a purposeful attempt to preserve the demonstrated efficiencies of behaviour modification within a less doctrinaire context and to incorporate the cognitive activities of the client within the effort to produce therapeutic change (Kendall & Hollon, 1979). Cognitive therapy is based on the underlying theoretical rationale that an individual's affect and behaviour are largely determined by the way in which he or she structures the world (Beck, 1963; Beck, Emery, & Greenberg, 1985). A person's cognitions (verbal or pictorial 'events' in the stream of consciousness) are based on attitudes or assumptions (schemata) developed from previous experiences (Beck, Freeman, & Associates, 1990). Cognitions are considered the most important links in the chain of events leading to disordered behaviour and psychological dysfunctions (Powell & Oei, 1991).

Three broad theoretical assumptions underlie cognitive therapy approaches. First, a person's thoughts, images, perceptions, and other cognitive mediating events are presumed to affect behaviour (Beck et al., 1985). This is especially true with children, who do not manifest rational thinking, and for whom feelings and images are as important as facts. Cognitive therapy with children recognises the influences and interdependencies of cognitive, affective, social, developmental, biological, and behavioural factors in the aetiology and remediation of psychopathology (Powell & Oei, 1991). The second assumption is that individuals are active participants in their own learning. Active participation comprises an important step towards mobilising the child's motivation and empowerment. Many therapists recognise the importance of adopting a therapeutic method where the child can actively participate and can learn to develop new cognitive processes to replace those that are maladaptive or absent (Powell & Oei, 1991). Third, it is accepted that the utility of cognitive constructs in efforts towards behaviour change must be empirically demonstrated (Hughes, 1988).

Cognitive–behavioural theoreticians and therapists are guided by several main principles (Kendall & Braswell, 1985):

1. Cognitive mediational processes are involved in human learning.

2. Thoughts, feelings, and behaviours are causally interrelated.
3. Cognitive activities such as expectations, self-statements, and attributions are important in understanding and predicting psychopathology and psychotherapeutic change.
4. Cognitions and behaviours are compatible: cognitive processes can be interpreted into behavioural paradigms, and cognitive techniques can be combined with behavioural procedures.
5. The task of the cognitive-behavioural therapist is to collaborate with the client to assess distorted or deficient cognitive processes and behaviours and to design new learning experiences to remediate the dysfunctional or deficient cognitions, behaviours, and affective patterns.

MAJOR COGNITIVE THEORETICIANS

In presenting some major trends in cognitive therapy, I shall briefly describe the main ideas of several people who centrally influenced cognitive therapy: Ellis, Beck, Meichenbaum, D'Zurilla, and Bandura.

In his therapeutic approach—rational emotive therapy—Ellis (1962) advocated teaching clients to examine the rationality of their beliefs, encouraging them to generate change. His treatment was based on verbal persuasion, arguments, and paradoxical and Socratic questioning for exploring his ideas. Ellis used cognitive structuring for the disputation of the distorted thought, viewing rationality as the primary mechanism of change.

Unlike Ellis, Beck was more interested in exploring the client's idiosyncratic meaning systems, emphasising the role of empiricism and encouraging clients to treat their beliefs as hypotheses to be tested (Hollon & Beck, 1994). In his therapeutic approach, Beck (1963, 1976) incorporated behavioural components aimed towards helping clients to practise the necessary skills. Beck taught his clients to achieve change systematically through methods such as monitoring, daily recording, self-talk, increasing awareness of emotions, and efforts to stop thinking and to change one's thoughts.

Meichenbaum (1979) initially conceptualised a cognition as a covert self-statement, a form of private speech that could be modified via modelling and repetition. His approach combined cognitive restructuring with training in verbal self-instruction and behavioural self-management techniques (Hollon & Beck, 1994). Meichenbaum based his therapy on the identification of internal self-talk, changing the present self-talk to one that helps overcome the problem, and practising internal dialogues.

D'Zurilla (Hollon & Beck, 1994) developed problem-solving training, which is designed to provide clients with a set of sequential procedures for dealing with problematic situations and interpersonal conflicts. This approach focused on decision-making skills. Attention to existing beliefs is limited, and the reliance is on more behavioural procedures such as rehearsal and role play in order to produce change.

Cognitive therapy also gained much from Bandura's (1977) social learning theory which described the role of expectancies in human behaviour. Bandura stated that people's expectations affect their behaviour and that the outcome of their behaviour affects their expectations, in a reciprocal process of influence. It is now widely believed that systematic, rational examination and manipulation of the client's thinking patterns results in goal-directed change in the client's functioning and behaviours (Graziano, 1978; Kazdin, 1979), just as the environment can reciprocally influence the person's thinking (Craighead, Meyer, & Craighead, 1985).

As can be seen from the above description, many techniques and strategies had been developed for the use of cognitive therapy with children, deriving both from behavioural therapy with children and from cognitive therapy with adults. What is missing in cognitive therapy with children is a broad theory for integrating those techniques and strategies into one integral theoretical framework.

GUIDELINES FOR THERAPISTS: COGNITIVE–BEHAVIOURAL INTERVENTIONS

At this point, we are ready to embark on the journey that comprises applying cognitive child interventions:

- Before applying cognitive therapy with children, carefully examine the kind of problems that the child presents. Is the most significant problem related to the child's thoughts, emotions, or behaviours?

- What kind of change is in the best interest of the child? Imparting lacking skills? Eliminating behaviour that occurs too frequently? Reducing anxiety that disturbs the child's functioning?
- Consider the possibility of applying cognitive therapy with the specific child. What kind of technique could be best suited to the child's age and cognitive stage?

SUMMARY

Cognitive therapy with children stems directly from behavioural therapy; therefore, classical, operant, and modelling learning are frequently applied with children. The development of cognitive therapy with children is highly rooted in Bandura's theory about the role of expectancies in one's learning and the capacity for expectancies to be successfully conditioned in therapy. In addition, cognitive child therapy derives from other theoreticians' conceptualisations about cognitive therapy with adults. Unlike adult cognitive therapy, however, which involves the rational modification of thoughts, the cognitive treatment of children is more concerned with teaching appropriate skills and applying certain techniques.

8

THE ROLE OF
DEVELOPMENTAL
LEVEL IN COGNITIVE
THERAPY WITH
CHILDREN

Traditional therapists continue to doubt the appropriateness and efficacy of cognitive treatments for children, due to the fact that cognitive therapy in adults depends largely on the client's ability to engage in philosophical disputation, logical analysis, and abstract thinking. Yet cognitive–behavioural therapy has been considered a promising treatment strategy for dysfunctional children (Dush, Hirt, & Schroeder, 1989; Gresham, 1981), as long as the therapist is able to adapt techniques to the children's developmental needs (Ronen, 1992). For example, young children and problem learners do not engage in cognitive-mediation strategies spontaneously; however, they can produce these strategies when provided with instruction in their use. Many children who do not generate memory strategies spontaneously can produce and benefit from these strategies when instructed to utilise them (Hughes, 1988).

The main deficiency in child cognitive therapy lies in the fact that there is no comprehensive theoretical model, as exists for adult therapy (Rossman, 1992). Rather, cognitive therapy with children consists of an umbrella term encompassing different treatment techniques that are offered in many different sequences and permutations, precluding comprehensive meta-analysis. Reviews of the research literature have emphasised the variance in outcomes across studies and the lack of agreement regarding the identification of subject, treatment, or methodological factors that increase effectiveness (Durlak, Fuhrman, & Lampman, 1991; Whalen, Henker, & Hinshaw, 1985). Only a little work has focused on developing broad-based assessment or treatment methods such as those existing for adults (Rossman, 1992). Most of the work being done with children either addresses one specific problem or makes use of one specific technique, instead of developing a general theoretical model to assess and address childhood disorders as well as to provide a framework for evaluating the proposed techniques.

The determination of a theoretical foundation for cognitive therapy with children necessitates some changes and an adaptation of the basic cognitive model to include assessment of developmental factors such as age, cognitive level, and the kind of problems referred which can contribute to the selection of the most suitable method of treatment (Ronen, 1993a, 1993b). Theoretical considerations have led to the hypothesis that children's cognitive developmental level would be the most important moderator in the efficacy of implementing cognitive therapy (Durlak et al., 1991; Dush et al., 1989) as well as in the genesis and maintenance of maladaptive and adaptive behaviour (Beidel & Turner, 1986). Dush et al. (1989) found a positive relationship between age and treatment outcome, where older children having more advanced cognitive skills benefited more from cognitive treatments. The best results were found for adolescents (aged 13 to 18 years), and good outcomes were also shown for pre-adolescents (aged 11 to 13), but only one-half the success rate was demonstrated with younger children (aged 5 to 11) (Durlak et al., 1991).

Contradictory findings exist with regard to cognitive therapy for young children. Children up to the age of 12 are considered to be in the concrete operational stage (Piaget, 1926) of their cognitive development, as manifested by their egocentricity and ability to deal with concrete simple notions but not with complex abstract ones. Nevertheless, it has been suggested that every child, no matter how young, can benefit from cognitive–behavioural therapy, provided only that the therapist is able to adapt the treatment to the child's personal cognitive style (Knell, 1993; Ronen, 1992).

Accepting that the treatment goals and procedures should be suited to the child's individual pace, as related to age and cognitive level (Ronen, 1995), any child can be expected to benefit from the process of cognitive therapy. Older children can develop cognitive strategies independently, whereas younger children need the therapist to develop strategies for them. Children with a high level of cognitive development can enjoy abstract and general strategies, whereas children with a low cognitive level will need specific, concrete strategies. Diagnostic procedures should also include an assessment of the child's attribution style in order to formulate appropriate interventions, in view of the fact that children with an internal attribution style can manage independently, whereas children with an external attribution style may need external control (Copeland, 1982; Ronen, 1992).

Cognitive therapy addresses children with externalising (e.g., hyperactive, aggressive, disruptive) and internalising (e.g., depressed, anxious) disorders differently. Externalising or under-controlled children (Achenbach, 1985) demonstrate difficulties in tolerating frustration, delaying gratification, keeping attention on target, or using problem-solving skills, and can be best treated using verbal methods directed towards imparting them with the lacking skills. Internalising or overcontrolled children, who have the necessary skills but misconstrue and misconceive social situations, can benefit best from a non-verbal therapeutic mode, especially exposure and experiencing. Kendall (1993) suggested that internalising children are limited to distorted thinking, whereas externalising children act without thinking or planning and lack careful information processing in situations in which thinking would be beneficial.

CHILDREN'S ABILITY TO LEARN

From birth children begin to learn, acquiring new cognitive skills each year. Even behaviours that appear very simple and natural such as toilet training, acquiring language, and learning to read and write involve cognitive skills.

In most modern countries, children initiate their studies even before entering school, through their years in nursery schools and kindergarten. As they begin school, children learn numbers and to write their names, then to read and to write. They may soon study classical literature (such as the Bible) that is written in a difficult and unfamiliar language. In many countries, children start learning a second language and have mastered basic mathematics before they reach the stage of early adolescence (i.e., before the age of 11). Thus, in the academic realm, children's ability to learn complicated subjects from a young age is very well accepted. Teachers and parents even tend to think that children learn more easily than adults (i.e., languages, computers).

Cognitive therapists argue that if a child can learn, he or she is a good partner for cognitive therapy (Ronen, 1992). Children even learn about the brain and the body, so why should they not learn how to change their way of thinking? If they can learn about the water cycle in nature and how their ears function, they can also learn how their thoughts elicit their emotions, and how their emotions are related to their behaviours. If there is an assumption that children cannot understand such concepts, then what is the explanation for children's achievements at school?

It is true that cognitive therapists must consider the fact that very young children are only able to deal with and understand concrete concepts. Therefore, cognitive therapy with young children, unlike cognitive therapy with adults, must be based not on changing irrational thinking but rather on translating the treatment's abstract goals (e.g., mediated thinking) and concepts (e.g., brain commands) into real, concrete notions. The use of simple situations that are familiar from day-to-day life enables children to comprehend and deal with these notions through play or art, in the same way that children can relate to television characters by referring to them as real-life figures.

Accordingly, every child, no matter how young, can benefit from cognitive therapy, provided only that the therapist meets two conditions. First, the therapist should be able to adapt the treatment to the child's personal cognitive style. Such adaptations include translation of abstract terms to concrete ones (e.g., 'automatic thought' becomes 'doing something without thinking about it'); utilisation of simple words (e.g., 'mediated thought' becomes 'a command or order that the brain sends to the body'); use of demonstrations, metaphors, and illustrations taken from the child's own day-to-day life (e.g., changing one's behaviour is likened to learning to ride a bicycle—one needs knowledge, desire, and time); and use of games and play for learning (e.g., controlling the mind can be taught through games relating to commander and soldiers, demonstrating who controls the situation). Second, the treatment goals and procedures should be suited to the child's individual pace, as related to age and cognitive level (Ronen, 1992). Accepting these conditions, any child can be expected to benefit from the process of cognitive therapy if the appropriate techniques are selected and adapted to children's individual differences. Chapter 9 will provide further examples of helpful metaphors and approaches to adapting specific cognitive techniques to children's developmental level.

GUIDELINES FOR THERAPISTS: THE CHILD'S DEVELOPMENTAL LEVEL

At this stage, we consider the child's developmental stage as a basis for decision making in selecting appropriate cognitive techniques:

- What do you know about the child's history of learning? Identify the child's developmental stage, cognitive level, and stage of perception.
- In view of the child's developmental abilities, should you conduct verbal or non-verbal therapy with the child? To make this decision, note the kind of concepts the child understands; how the child responds to play, imagery, or art; and the externalising or internalising nature of the child's problem.
- Note specific features of the child's ability to learn (style and contents) that can be utilised in therapy. What kind of examples, stories, or metaphors does the child discuss? What are the hobbies or interests that the child has mastered and enjoys? How does the child describe his or her understanding of day-to-day experiences? What words or terms does the child use?

SUMMARY

Unlike the traditional question 'Is cognitive therapy adequate for children', this chapter raises the question 'At which age is cognitive therapy most effective?', or rather, 'What is the best way to apply cognitive therapy with children at different developmental levels?'. It is a misconception to think that someone can be too young or too lacking in skills to benefit from cognitive therapy. Instead, efforts should be invested in identifying the most effective way to apply cognitive therapy to children. It is important to understand that children can learn, that they are rational, and can even be taught complicated notions if explanations are provided in simple words.

Unlike traditional therapies which each suggest one way to solve children's problems, cognitive therapy is characterised by its proposal of many techniques, strategies, and methods for changing children's disorders. Responsibility lies with the therapist, therefore, to find the best means for working with the individual child suffering from a specific, personal, problem.

9

APPLYING COGNITIVE TECHNIQUES TO CHILDREN

A wide range of cognitive–behavioural therapy strategies exists for children, many of which emphasise the manipulation of behavioural responses such as modelling, sequential rehearsal, and skills training. The underlying target of therapy, however, consistently focuses on the cognitive distortions and deficiencies that surround the behavioural events (Powell & Oei, 1991). Cognitive techniques have been proffered as a means of remediating factors that prevent youngsters from exhibiting behaviours in their repertoire while also promoting generalisation because of their reduced reliance on environmental contingencies to maintain behaviour (Karoly & Kanfer, 1982; Kendall & Braswell, 1982).

All cognitive interventions attempt to produce change by influencing thinking (Mahoney, 1977). The techniques are designed to identify, reality-test, and correct the distorted conceptualisations and the dysfunctional beliefs (schemata) underlying these cognitions. By re-evaluating and correcting their thinking, clients learn to master problems and situations which they previously considered insuperable (Beck, Rush, Shaw, & Emery, 1979).

Cognitive techniques are aimed at delineating and testing the client's specific misconceptions and maladaptive assumptions. Therefore, the client is taught: to monitor negative automatic thoughts (cognitions); to recognise the connection between cognition, affect, and behaviour; to examine the evidence for and against the distorted automatic thoughts; to substitute more reality-oriented interpretations for these biased cognitions; and to learn to identify and alter the dysfunctional beliefs which predispose the experiences (Beck et al., 1979).

In this chapter, I shall focus on techniques that are connected and being used especially in cognitive therapy. I shall not mention techniques such as role playing, redefinition, rehearsal, relaxation, etc., not because they are unimportant but because I believe the readers are already familiar with them from behavioural methods. I shall provide an overview and illustrations for the following techniques: self-instructional training, changing automatic thoughts, the continuum tool, imagination, problem-solving skills, cognitive structuring, self-control methods (self-recording, self-evaluation, and self-reinforcement), and stress inoculation training.

SELF-INSTRUCTIONAL TRAINING

Self-instructional training is one of the most popular cognitive techniques for working with children and has been applied to a broad range of childhood disorders. Adults are taught to use self-talk to encourage themselves when performing a task they find difficult, in order to change the way they feel about it. Yet adults often perceive the self-talk as artificial and objectionable. With children, self-talk is much more natural; they frequently talk to themselves during play, while starting to learn new skills, or when they feel bored.

The influence of Vygotsky, Luria, and Mischel on self-instructional training has been significant. Vygotsky's (1962) work provided the concepts of the development of language control over behaviour and the shift from talking aloud to internal self-talk. Vygotsky proposed that the internalisation of verbal commands is a crucial step in a child's establishment of voluntary control over behaviour (Kendall & Braswell, 1985). Luria's (1961) work traced the developmental changes in children's ability to regulate their behaviour, by the shift from adult verbalisations to self-talk. Mischel's (1974) contribution stemmed from his research on the ability of children to delay gratification and overcome temptation through the use of verbal coping strategies (i.e., self-talk).

There are several ways to apply self-instructional training with children. In the non-interactive method, the therapist merely tells the child what to do and/or what to say, and the child is instructed to repeat the activity and verbalisation. In the interactive method, self-instruction is taught as a skill on a par with self-control techniques (described below) such as self-monitoring, self-evaluation and/or self-reinforcement (Kanfer, 1970, 1977). The third method employs a process of modelling, imitation, and execution: the trainer first models the desired actions while speaking the self-instructions aloud; the trainer then says the self-instructions aloud with the child, as the child carries out the actions; and, finally, the child states the self-instructions while accomplishing the required task.

An integral part of teaching self-talk to children is the need to be sincere, rather than lie to oneself. Children should be cautioned not to say 'I'm not afraid' when they are frightened, but instead to use self-talk in order to cope with the fear, as in, 'I am afraid, but I can survive. It is not so frightening. I can overcome!' Children take these instructions literally, and they practise talking to themselves very easily. The need for parents and teachers to be forewarned about this technique, however, can be gleaned from the following example from my clinical practice:

A mother of one of my clients called me, frightened. She reported that her son entered his room, talking to himself, saying, 'I'm afraid' and then answering himself, 'No, I'm not. I am brave.' She complained that I had caused her child to hallucinate.

Rose and Edelson (1987, p. 205) gave an example of the use of self-instructions from a group therapy session with children. The first stage involved cognitive rehearsal of what one girl should tell herself while working on a puzzle:

Group leader: Okay Romy, . . . give it a try in a loud whisper, what are you thinking?
Romy: First, I have to organise this mess . . . I'll make a plan . . . I just better go a little more slowly.

Meichenbaum (1979) also used self-talk for stress inoculation in children, and Kanfer, Karoly, and Newman (1975) used self-talk for decreasing fear of the dark in young children.

CHANGING AUTOMATIC THOUGHTS

Beck's main technique (Beck et al., 1979; Beck, Emery, & Greenberg, 1985) was to change habitual, automatic thoughts to mediated, more adaptive ones. Although it seems very complicated, children can learn to change automatic thoughts if the therapist uses the right metaphors and techniques. To explain the concept of automatic thoughts to young children, I often use the metaphor of a flowing river.

> I ask the child to draw a river in the direction in which it flows. Then I ask: 'If we want to change the direction of the water, what can we do?' I illustrate the answer on the drawing: 'We need to dig a new canal or ditch, and to build a dam over the old one. Up until now the river would automatically flow that way. Now it can flow in a new direction—this way. This is what happens with the brain's old, automatic commands and how we can change them into a new, mediated one.'

One technique I often employ is to ask children to write down daily an example of habitual negative thoughts. ('Write down an example of something that happened to you. What is the wrong, bad interpretation you can give this situation?') At first, to practise the method, the children can use hypothetical ('pretend or imaginary') examples, or the parents can provide examples of events that elicited negative automatic thinking in their children, and the children need only practise verbalising and recording their own 'good' and 'bad' interpretations of the event. After such practice, I ask them to record real examples from their day-to-day life. A chart along the lines of the sample in Table 6 is helpful.

Table 6: Sample self-recording chart for automatic negative thoughts

What happened?	The bad thought I had	How I felt	What I did	Can I give a good explanation
A child laughed	He always laughs at me	Terrible	I cried	The child was happy so he laughed

Following the generation of the possible 'good
the event, the child could also be encouraged to ex╻
she would then feel and what he or she might then dᴗ.

THE CONTINUUM TOOL

The aim of the continuum method is to help the child attain a more
realistic perception of the problem, and improve the child's self-
evaluation by teaching how to rate himself or herself in relation to:
others (e.g., peers); a different time in life (e.g., last month); wishes
(e.g., the ideal situation or desired behaviour); a different component in functioning (e.g., extent of tics in English versus math class
versus recess). An example of the therapist's usage of the continuum tool for fears would be:

> *Therapist:* You say your fear last evening was 10, on a scale of 1 to 10.
> What was it like during the night?
> *Boy:* 10.
> *T:* Was it the same all day yesterday?
> *B:* Yes.
> *T:* And how would you rate your fear today?
> *B:* It's much worse.
> *T:* Oh, it's not the same—it's higher today? If the maximum is 10,
> and today is higher, then maybe we should rethink yesterday's
> rating? Maybe yesterday it was only 9? Could it be?
> *B:* Well, yes, I guess so.
> *T:* You said today was much worse. So maybe you could even
> reduce yesterday's rating to 8?
> *B:* Yes, it could have been 8.

These comparative ratings help the client move from a basic holistic view of 'all or nothing', which causes one's self-perception as 'a
nothing, a failure' to be changed into a view of oneself as lying
somewhere in a good position along a continuum of other people
or situations.

Christine Padesky and Kathleen Mooney, in their Center for
Cognitive Therapy in California, use the continuum in many different ways as a treatment technique for adults. Children can

also learn to use a continuum if we introduce it simply. For example:

> With a very shy girl who felt she was fat and avoided going to the swimming pool because she was ashamed to take off her clothes, I asked her to list all of the children in her class. We then created a continuum where 0 represented 'fat and ugly' and 100 represented looking 'like a model'. At first she rated herself as the ugliest girl in the class, putting herself on 0. Then she remembered one girl who was uglier, so she had to move herself to 5 and put her classmate on 0. Shortly, she saw that there were very few girls on 100 and very few on 0, so she moved herself to 30 and placed most of the girls between 30 and 50.
>
> Another way we utilised the continuum was to break up the concept of ugly into components and to rate each of them separately. Soon we discovered that relating to her weight she gave herself a 2, but there were many parts of her body which rated between 80 and 90. For example, she thought her hair was 90, her eyes were 80, her nose was 82, her mouth was 70, etc. Again, the continuum method changed her holistic view of herself as a worthless 'nothing'.
>
> Still another usage of the continuum was to view her looks as only one component of her self-evaluation. Even if she initially rated her looks as a 0, she viewed herself differently in terms of her manners, brains, social skills, etc.

IMAGINATION

Many self-control methods make use of imagination as a way to overcome fears, anxieties, or other kinds of difficulties. Adults need to be trained to use imagination and to understand that this is a preliminary step in overcoming *in vivo*. Children, in contrast, deal with imagination in a very concrete manner, and also use imagination naturally in their day-to-day lives, and enjoy doing so. When a child is afraid that a wild animal might enter his or her bed, there is no sense in explaining that no wild animals prowl the city. Rather, teaching the child to draw a gun or sword for protection is much more effective. Teaching children to use imagination to pretend that they are television figures or that they have special powers is very effective for overcoming obstacles in their lives. For example:

Pretend you are Superman, and this boy comes over to tease you. What would you do? How do you think you—as Superman—could get rid of him?

Or:

Let's imagine that you won a TV game show and got tickets to a wonderful place far away in another country. Try to describe yourself in that place. What do you look like while you're there? What are you thinking about there? How do you behave? Who is there with you?

PROBLEM-SOLVING SKILLS

Problem-solving skills are needed to function in social, interpersonal contexts and might be seen as one's social understanding of interpersonal conflicts. Spivack and Shure (1974) reported the development of a series of interpersonal cognitive problem-solving skills said to be associated with impaired behavioural adjustment. Those skills included sensitivity to interpersonal problems, causal thinking, readiness to consider the consequences of behaviour, the capacity to generate a list of possible solutions, and the ability to produce step-by-step means for reaching specific goals.

Children can first learn problem solving as a game, especially as a group assignment, and then they can start applying it to their personal lives. It is easiest to teach children these skills using Kendall and Braswell's (1985) modelling methods: (a) the therapist instructs the children in what to do while they only give the examples; (b) the children are given instruction cards to be read aloud for directing themselves; (c) the children can then give themselves instructions while the therapist supervises them; and (d) the children can practise the whole process delineated by the problem-solving model without receiving either oral or written instructions but rather by instructing themselves.

A clinical example may illustrate the technique:

'Yossi' was an aggressive boy who was teased in elementary school and who tended to respond immediately with aggressive outbursts and hitting. To teach him problem-solving skills to serve him in these repeated situations, Yossi was first asked to generate the possible alternatives he could have conceivably demonstrated in response to another boy's teasing. Yossi suggested:

1. To stay quiet.
2. To tease him back, insulting him and using bad words.
3. To hit him.
4. To go tell the teacher.

The next step was to ask Yossi to examine the probable outcomes, with the therapist's help and guidance, including the advantages and disadvantages for each alternative:

1. If I stay quiet, the boy will think I'm a coward. But, if he sees I don't answer, maybe he'll stop bothering me, and then the teacher will be happy because she'll see I'm a kid who can control himself.
2. If I tease him back, the fight will get bigger and bigger.
3. If I hit him, he'll see that I'm strong and will learn a lesson. On the other hand, the teacher will punish me.
4. If I go tell the teacher, the boy will think I'm a tattletale, but the teacher will punish him, not me.

In the next stage of training, Yossi was asked to reiterate his goal. He stated it was to have the boy stop teasing him. In that case, alternatives 2 and 3 would not solve his problem. He was left with two options: staying quiet or telling the teacher. In the next stage of treatment, Yossi was encouraged to go back to the schoolyard and classroom, experiment with the various alternatives, evaluate their effectiveness in solving his problem, and return to the therapy with some conclusions for discussion. The aim of this intervention is to teach children the model—how to raise and analyse different alternatives for behaviour in order to solve problems. Sometimes hitting or teasing back may be the answer, once the cost–benefit ratio is examined.

COGNITIVE STRUCTURING

Cognitive structuring is a method based on the assumption that clients' problems are often a result of magical thinking or irrational ideas. Some of these ideas lead to self-condemnation, others to anger, etc. The therapist helps the client to examine these thoughts and change them. The major technique consists of verbal persuasion and Socratic questioning. The following example uses cognitive restructuring for a child with a speech deficit:

A 9-year-old boy, 'Jonathan', suffered from a stuttering problem. Jonathan insisted he could not control his stuttering, and that he stuttered because he did not know how to speak properly. Using cognitive structuring, I attempted to show him that he stuttered only in certain situations that aroused tension and anxiety; therefore, he did know how to speak and even had a certain extent of control over his problem.

Therapist: How did you evaluate your speech today in our meeting? Did you stutter?
Jonathan: No, almost not at all.
T: When you talked to your mother on the way here, did you stutter?
J: No.
T: Do you stutter when you're with your best friend?
J: Almost never.
T: So there are lots of people and situations when you don't. Doesn't that mean that you know how to talk properly? And if it means you know how, maybe not knowing isn't the problem. Maybe the problem is related to the way you put pressure on yourself and upset yourself in certain situations or with certain people, and that's what interferes with the fluency of your speech?

Cognitive structuring is a method directed towards building a new perception of the world instead of the old misconceptions. Through cognitive structuring, children learn certain general principles such as problem solving, creative processing, or frustration tolerance as a result of learning to work systematically on a variety of complex tasks. In this procedure cognitive distortions or illogical statements adhered to by the child are identified and replaced. Rose and Edelson (1987, p. 205) presented the steps for using this technique in group work. First the group must evaluate the cognitive distortion and replace it with logical or self-enhancing self-statements:

Lavette: Everyone at school thinks I'm weird. Maybe I am.
Lynn: What do the rest of you think—is Lavette weird?
Sandy: I don't think she's weird . . .

Other steps are cognitive modelling of the new response, cognitive rehearsal, and self-reinforcement. Rose and Edelson (1987) summed up their suggested steps for cognitive restructuring in groups:

—Providing rational training in the basic concepts.
—Identifying self-defeating and self-enhancing statements.
—Logically disputing self-defeating thought patterns.
—Shifting from self-defeating to self-enhancing statements.
—Modelling the shift to self-enhancing cognitions.
—Rehearsing the shift to self-enhancing cognitions.
—Group feedback.
—Fading.

SELF-CONTROL METHODS

One of the basic techniques necessary for cognitive therapy is self-control, which comprises self-recording, self-evaluation, and self-reinforcement (Kanfer, 1970, 1977).

Self-recording

In light of cognitive therapy's aim to teach individuals how they behave and how they wish to change, a necessary first step in treatment consists of learning to become aware of and recognise their belief systems, emotions, and behaviours. Most treatment strategies, therefore, initially include self-recording methods (also termed self-observation or self-monitoring), where clients are taught to maintain records or conduct a diary of their own behaviour. Self-monitoring practices can be used during the assessment process to identify baseline functioning, during intervention to examine progress, and following the termination of treatment as a tool to enhance the maintenance of gains.

With children, self-observation has a special function. As children do not refer themselves to therapy and most often do not recognise the need for therapy, self-monitoring can present them with concrete evidence that a problem exists. Although self-observation is a difficult skill to master, it can be taught to children (Gross & Drabman, 1982). Self-recording methods should be introduced to children through the use of metaphors and by giving simple examples. In general, I find Kanfer's concept of 'acting like a scientist' (Kanfer & Schefft, 1988) extremely useful with children:

> Let's imagine you are a scientist. Just as a researcher carefully studies cells through a microscope, your subject for research will be your own behaviour. You will observe the way you behave and keep records.

In order to teach children self-monitoring skills, this method must be practised in the therapy session, first devising simple, individualised observation sheets and then providing supervision in their completion. The more specific and simple items are the most conducive to children's cooperation and success. Devising direct questions for the child to answer (e.g., Did X behaviour occur or not?) is preferable to free observation tasks. Examples of direct questions would be:

> Did I succeed in concentrating during the first period of the school day?
> Did I ask permission to talk in class?
> Did I hold my hands down and avoid hitting other children at school?

Or:

> Did I concentrate in school today?
> Was it difficult?
> How difficult was it on a scale of 0–10?
> In which class period was it easiest to concentrate?

Whenever possible, positive forms ('Did I talk politely today?') should replace negative forms ('Was I rude today?'). Similarly, measuring an increase or progress ('How many dry nights did I have during the last week?') is preferable to measuring a decrease ('How many nights did I wet the bed during the last week?').

The use of self-recording for assessment often leads to a decrease in children's disruptive behaviour, highlighting this technique's usefulness both as a preliminary phase of cognitive treatment and as a method for behavioural change.

Self-evaluation

Evaluating oneself necessitates the ability to hold some standard criteria for comparing oneself to others or to other situations. Such an ability appears problematic for children due to their egocentric functioning and perceptions of the environment. Yet, self-evaluation can be taught to children if it is taught in a manner they can conceive and comprehend.

The use of concrete examples can facilitate children's self-evaluations. For instance:

> I like to use a ladder to show children how they can climb from one stage to another. With small children an actual ladder is best; older children respond well to a drawing of a ladder. 'If we decide that not using curse words at all (talking very politely) is the highest rung of the ladder, and swearing all day long is the lowest rung, where do you think you can stand today? Did you talk very politely? Politely, but not all the time?'

The use of a continuum or scale can be effective in self-evaluation, especially when comparing present and past functioning. For example, anxious children can evaluate themselves today as compared with yesterday: 'If 10 is the most fearful situation for you, and yesterday you rated yourself as being 8, how much would you give yourself today?'

In my clinical experience, I found children to be very proud and happy to cooperate in using self-evaluation methods. They seemed to feel that they were being treated as grown-ups and enjoyed making decisions for themselves. Again, self-evaluation is an integral part of the assessment process, but teaching children to evaluate themselves also constitutes a good method for behavioural change. By fostering children's perceptions of their behaviour as something that can be changed, rather than something absolute, change is already in progress.

Self-reinforcement

Self-reinforcement comprises the third part of the basic self-control model (Kanfer & Schefft, 1988). All people should learn to reinforce themselves, as an important step towards becoming independent. With children, this method helps to shift children's attention from concrete reinforcements to symbolic ones. Self-reinforcement also helps to develop self-confidence and improve self-image, especially for shy or perfectionist children who find it difficult to compliment themselves.

I find it easier to teach self-reinforcement to children than to adults. With young children, I keep a box of rewards in my room. Children know that by the end of the session they need to make up their minds: 'Do I deserve reinforcement? Do I deserve a small or a big one?' Many times children will tell me, 'I didn't succeed but I really tried hard. Could I pick something out, just to make me feel better?' (a comfort reinforcement). Or a child may say, 'I didn't really put in any effort today, and I know I don't deserve anything, but I like this sticker. Could you put it aside and keep it for me for next week?'

Often parents find it difficult to observe their children's dilemma when choosing their own reinforcements. When parents are tempted to 'help' by telling their children what they should or should not select, they prevent children from making up their own minds and learning to reach decisions based on personal tastes, preferences, or moods.

After only a short term using concrete reinforcements, I try to teach every child to use symbolic reinforcement by asking each one to 'Write down a compliment to yourself' or 'Write down one good thing about yourself every night'. At first it is difficult, but soon children learn the skill of symbolic self-reinforcement and even enjoy it. Again, it is important to practise these skills during the therapy session, and to enlist parents' help with young children. For example, parents could be instructed to write down a compliment to the child each time the child succeeds in a given assignment. The child could then be asked to write: 'How did I feel when my parent(s) complimented me? Do I agree with my parent(s)?'

STRESS INOCULATION TRAINING

One cognitive approach that would appear to provide an ideal, comprehensive conceptual format for addressing children's disorders is stress inoculation training (SIT). This was developed as a treatment for management of anxiety, anger, and pain (Meichenbaum, 1985; Novaco, 1979). The focus of SIT is to help individuals develop and employ a repertoire of skills that enables them to cope with a variety of stressful situations.

The training starts with the conceptualisation phase, where the problem and its components are identified. Meichenbaum (1985) emphasised the need in this phase to establish the therapeutic relationship with the individual, to collect data and relevant information as to the particular pattern of deficits and strengths, and to reconceptualise the individual's problem as one that is amenable to change. One of the important features of this phase is the need for the client to understand the problem—an element upon which every cognitive therapy is based. Meichenbaum suggested that many individuals enter therapy with a confused understanding of their problems. It is assumed that by reconceptualising the problem as consisting of a variety of stages or factors, the individual will view his or her difficulties as being more amenable to change. Problems are translated into challenges to solve proactively, rather than stressful situations to react to negatively.

With children there is a need to emphasise environmental factors. For example, instead of focusing on the nature of anxiety or stress, the therapist could concentrate on showing the child the negative attention he or she received from peers following the negative behaviours (Magg & Kotlash, 1994). Children should be taught to understand the role of classmates' play in maintaining an inappropriate behaviour or in preventing the performance or acquisition of appropriate responses. The target youngster then becomes a collaborator in helping to design environmental contingencies that would make the appropriate behaviour more likely to occur.

The second phase directs the client's focus onto his or her internal dialogue while facing the problem (e.g., 'I'm scared. I can't do it. I'm sure I'm going to fail'). In the coping statement phase, the client is then taught coping sentences (e.g., 'I can do it') to help overcome the problem. At first the client tries to use coping statements in the therapeutic setting, and then gradually these statements are used in the natural environment, in increasingly difficult situations. Meichenbaum and Goodman (1971) demonstrated the self-statement and behavioural rehearsal phases for SIT, proposing the following sequence:

1. The trainer models the task and talks aloud while the child observes (overt cognitive modelling).
2. The child performs the task, giving self-instruction aloud and getting assistance from the trainer (overt external guidance).
3. The child performs the task aloud without assistance.
4. The trainer models the same task but whispers the statements (faded overt modelling), and the child rehearses whispering to himself or herself without guidance.
5. The trainer performs the task using internal talk and the child models the same.

GUIDELINES FOR THERAPISTS: DECISION MAKING REGARDING TECHNIQUES

There are many available cognitive techniques to help the therapist help the child. The problem lies in choosing the most effective techniques for a specific child:

- Does the child use self-talk naturally in conversation? Do you think the child would agree to use self-instructions?
- Is it important for the child to appear as if he or she is independent and can make his or her own decisions? If so, you can teach the child how to make his or her own decision to control the mind and change automatic thoughts.
- Does the child compare himself or herself to others and feel inferior, or unable to cope? If so, try to use the continuum technique.
- Can the child concentrate, think systematically, and have the patience to learn systematic problem-solving methods?
- Can you identify disturbing misconceptions in the child that hinder progress? If so, use cognitive structuring for changing those misconceptions.
- Does the child lack self-control skills? If so, try teaching the child self-observation, self-evaluation, and self-reinforcement.

SUMMARY

This chapter presented several popular techniques for applying cognitive therapy to children. Most of the proposed techniques are in use for working with adults and have been adapted for work with children. The therapist has a range of options, from verbal techniques (self-instructions, changing automatic thoughts, cognitive structuring), writing or drawing techniques (drawing continuum), imagination techniques (creative imagination, use of metaphors or guided imagery), self-control methods (self-observation, self-evaluation, and self-reinforcement), to a combination of techniques into a systematic problem-solving model or stress inoculation training programme. All of the presented techniques aim at changing automatic thoughts, constructing more appropriate ways of thinking, and attaining a more balanced way of looking at oneself and one's world.

10

APPLYING COGNITIVE TECHNIQUES TO CHILDHOOD DISORDERS

In this chapter I shall address several predominant childhood disturbances in terms of the cognitive techniques that have been applied to their treatment by researchers and therapists: anxiety disorders, hyperactivity and impulsivity, depression, and aggressive disorders.

TREATING ANXIETY DISORDERS

Studies of cognitive behavioural treatment for childhood anxiety have focused on night-time fears, fear of dental/medical procedures, and test anxiety—the vast majority of these being clinical case studies or small samples (e.g., Kanfer, Karoly, & Newman, 1975; Ronen, 1993d). One of the only serious empirical works in this area (Kendall, 1994) has suggested that thoughts relating to fears of being threatened or evaluated by others are common in anxious children. Most of the small-sample studies have reported treatment success compared to control groups, when using a coping skills approach that combines self-instructional techniques with behavioural techniques such as *in-vivo* exposure, imagery, relaxation, and contingent rewards. Kanfer et al. (1975) used self-control procedures to treat children's night-time fears and presented good results for the group that used self-statements. They suggested that the self-statement using a competence statement (i.e., self-instructions to 'act like a brave boy [or girl]') had the greatest impact on fear reduction due to its association with expectations of social- and self-approval based on past experiences. Ronen (1993d) presented a successful treatment of sleep terror disorders using self-control methods combining self-talk, self-evaluation, thought-prevention, and imagery. Kendall (1994) presented his study as the first randomised clinical trial improving the effectiveness of cognitive–behavioural therapy for childhood anxiety disorders.

Graziano, Mooney, Hurber, and Ignasiak (1979) treated fearful children in an intervention involving five weekly sessions, with the first and last sessions for assessment and the three middle sessions devoted to instructions and discussions. Children were instructed in relaxation techniques ('Lie down and relax your muscles'), imagery techniques ('Choose a pleasant memory'), and coping self-statements ('I know I am able to overcome it').

The limited number of cognitive treatments addressing the problem of anxiety makes it difficult to reach final conclusions in relation to the efficacy of cognitive therapy with anxious children. Preliminary studies propose that the treatment could eliminate the anxiety as well as increase coping behaviour, but our knowledge in this area still needs to be extended.

TREATING HYPERACTIVITY AND IMPULSIVITY

One of the most frequent problems that disturbs teachers and educators is impulsiveness or hyperactivity among children. Children who display general difficulties in controlling their behaviour have been described as 'acting without thinking' (Kendall & Braswell, 1985), emphasising their deficiencies in thinking and planning abilities.

Many behavioural and cognitive studies address hyperactivity. Their common characteristic is the focus on attempting to teach the child generic cognitive strategies both for solving academic and cognitive problems and for successfully negotiating interpersonal exchanges (Hughes, 1988). Some intervention programmes are directed towards teaching the child self-directive cues to cognitively 'slow down' or in some way to increase the response latency interval. In these programmes the therapist teaches the child to repeat self-instructive phrases (e.g., 'Stop! Look! Think!') at appropriate times. The self-directive statements serve as cues or prompts to facilitate adherence to the problem-solving tactics. Several kinds of self-statements are useful for impulsive children (Kendall & Braswell, 1985): identification of the problem (What do I see here? What kind of work are they asking me to do?); specification of the strategies to be used (I should read it again carefully); attention-focusing statements (Oh, I have to concentrate, I missed something); self-rewarding statements (I really did well this time); and statements designed to assist the child in coping with ineffectual efforts (I missed, but I'll try again and then it might go better). Modelling has also been used for hyperactive children, where the therapist demonstrates an action and the child repeats it gradually.

Kendall and Braswell's (1985) training included problem solving, instructional training, behavioural contingencies, modelling, role play, and sometimes training in the identification of feelings in self and others. Other programmes train children in more complex problem-solving models; for example, Urbain (in Kendall & Braswell, 1985) included four stages in his training of children with attention-deficit/hyperactivity disorder:

1. *Problem identification:* The sensitivity to identify feelings instead of avoiding, denying, or acting impulsively when dealing with the problem.
2. *Alternative thinking:* The ability to generate multiple alternative solutions to a given interpersonal situation.
3. *Consequential thinking:* The capacity to foresee immediate and more long-term information in the decision-making process.
4. *Means–end thinking:* The ability to elaborate or plan a series of specific actions to attain a given goal and use a realistic time framework in implementing steps towards that goal.

Kendall, Padawear, Zupan, and Braswell (in Kendall & Braswell, 1985) have developed a self-control manual for impulsive children. The manual presents a 12-session format of exercises which has been found to be effective. The sessions involve teaching the child self-instructional procedures via modelling while working on a variety of intrapersonal and interpersonal problem-solving tasks.

The initial tasks are psycho-educational and are designed to resemble non-stressful class assignments. Gradually the tasks change into interpersonal play situations and the appropriate use of self-instructions.

In contrast to the problem of anxiety, much work has been conducted in the cognitive treatment of hyperactive and impulsive disorders. It seems that cognitive therapy could be seen as the treatment of choice for these children. By learning cognitive and self-control methods, not only can disturbances be prevented in some children, but also those youngsters who already exhibit hyperactivity and impulsivity can improve their general behaviour, learn to adapt themselves better to their environment, and gradually decrease medications.

TREATING DEPRESSION

Only during recent decades has awareness been increased to the phenomenon of depression among children, not as a temporary mood disorder but as a problem needing systematic treatment. Similarities have been found between depression in childhood and adulthood (Hughes, 1988). In Kendall's recent work (1994) on anxieties, similar components of depression and anxiety have emerged, suggesting the comorbidity of these two childhood disorders.

Depression has been one of the main disorders targeted by cognitive therapy for adults. Cognitive treatment of adult depression attempts to change the thinking patterns that produce the depressive symptoms. Depressed persons have a systematically negative bias in their thinking that causes them to have a negative view of themselves, the world, and the future.

Cognitive interventions for depressed children have focused on improving children's social skills and fostering participation in social activities. Hughes (1988) presented an intervention training consisting of 30 sessions lasting 20 to 30 minutes over a period of 15 weeks. Five steps were emphasized: the rationale for skilled behaviour, modelling of skills, verbal or behavioural rehearsal, feedback, and homework assignments to practise skills with others.

Rhem (1977) applied Kanfer's (1977) self-control model (based on the training of self-control skills including self-monitoring, self-evaluation, and self-reinforcement) to depressive children, using a three-phase intervention design. Most treatments of children within a cognitive framework have highlighted acting-out disorders, whereas Rhem's work brings into focus a new area (acting-in disorders) that offers much hope for the future. In contrast to adults, where the treatment of depression has been a main influence in the development of cognitive therapy, treating childhood depression is still a relatively new domain that needs to be developed. In sum, cognitive treatments of childhood depression seem promising, but further clinical and empirical work are necessary.

TREATING AGGRESSIVE DISORDERS

Aggressive and antisocial behaviours comprise one of the most frequent childhood problems referred to therapy. Aggressive children are viewed as suffering from deficiencies in social cognition, social skills deficits, and adjustment difficulties (Spivack & Shure, 1974). The need has also been cited to enhance aggressive children's role-taking abilities—in other words, their capacity to take the role or point of view of another person and to recognise others' perceptions, thoughts, and feelings (Hughes, 1988). Treating aggressive disorders involves not only problem-solving methods, but also the imparting of social skills, training in assertive behaviours, and working towards increasing one's self-efficacy and outcome expectancies. Intervention programmes also usually include self-instructional training and anger control techniques.

Lochman, Nelson, and Sims (1981) combined several techniques in their 10-session group training. Session 1 promoted self-awareness by noting similarities and differences among group members in physical, behavioural, and emotional cues. Session 2 explored children's reactions to cooperating with and being controlled by others. Session 3 concentrated on problem identification. Session 4 focused on generating alternative solutions to problems. Sessions 5 and 6 evaluated the solution by identifying the available outcomes. Session 7 increased sensitivity to the arousal of anger. Session 8 taught self-talk. Session 9 modelled techniques. Sessions 10 and 12 were devoted to integrating and practising the learned methods.

It seems as if cognitive therapy has much to propose in the area of aggressiveness. In the past, attention has been given to aggressive behaviour, yet angry, frustrating, and violent thoughts and emotions were neglected. A long-term effect for reducing aggressiveness could only be achieved by changing one's thoughts and emotions, and behaviours as well, indicating the suitability of cognitive treatments.

GUIDELINES FOR THERAPISTS: THE APPLICATION OF TECHNIQUES TO DIFFERENT CHILDHOOD DISORDERS

This chapter presents examples of cognitive treatments for different disorders, to serve as a starting point for the following questions:

- From the available list of techniques for the specific disorder exhibited by the referred child, which do you think are best suited to this individual child's problems?
- From what you know about the child, determine the kind of therapeutic mode that would be most appropriate for him or her: verbal, imagination, play, or other? How can you apply the techniques offered to this specific child's optimal mode of treatment?
- How can you motivate the child to carry out the specific therapeutic assignment? Think of the best way to present the technique to the child. Can you translate it into a metaphor or a game?

SUMMARY

Cognitive therapy allows for a range of techniques for different kinds of problems and personalities. The techniques are only a tool in achieving the aim of the treatment, which is helping children to change. The challenge for the therapist lies in two main areas: one, to select the most effective technique for changing the specific disorder; and two, to translate the techniques into the kind of communication that will be appropriate and motivating for the child, whether in verbal, imagination, or play techniques.

III

APPLYING COGNITIVE DEVELOPMENTAL THERAPY WITH CHILDREN

INTRODUCTION: TRENDS IN CHILDREN'S COGNITIVE THERAPY

Two main approaches have influenced the development of children's cognitive therapy: one is basic behavioural therapy, and the other is cognitive therapy for adults, rooted in Beck's and Ellis's formulations.

The behavioural approach, as an empirical, consistent means of intervention, emphasises the importance of basing therapy on: the results of assessment of the problem; the role of contemporaneous determinants of behaviour; the need to adapt different treatments to different problems; the evaluation of treatment outcomes; and the specification of treatment procedures (Hughes, 1993). This trend might best be characterised by Kanfer's six thinking rules for therapists (Kanfer & Schefft, 1988):

- Think behaviour (instead of concentrating on problems)
- Think solution (instead of causes)
- Think positive (rather than focusing on deficits)
- Think in small steps (instead of long-term outcomes)
- Think flexible (instead of continuing to do the same thing)
- Think future (instead of past)

The second approach, cognitive therapy for adults, is based on Beck's and Ellis's orientations. This approach emphasises: the formulation of psychological problems in terms of incorrect premises and a proneness to distorted imaginary experiences; the role of cognition in personal dysfunction; and the underlying theoretical rationale that an individual's affect and behaviour are largely determined by the way in which he or she structures the world, and that attitudes or assumptions are developed from previous experiences (Beck, Rush, Shaw, & Emery, 1979; Ellis, 1958, 1962).

Cognitive therapy with children does not relate to the theory underlying the intervention (e.g., personal repertoire, belief system, irrational or automatic way of thinking, schema, need to change one's thoughts and understand one's emotional response); rather, the treatment emphasises the techniques that are derived from the theory, due to the misconception that being a child means one cannot think rationally, analyse behaviour, or identify abstract concepts such as thoughts or emotions. Theoretical concepts central to adult treatment are seen as inappropriate under the assumption that children need to be taught 'how to do things' via a systematic learning of techniques and strategies.

Forehand and Wierson (1993) claimed that the practice of borrowing from the adult cognitive model for the application to children has ignored developmental theory and has hindered the matching of techniques to children's specific needs, problems, and characteristics, as unique from those of adults.

Part III of this book suggests that the lack of a clear cognitive theoretical model for children underlies the current inconsistent application of different cognitive techniques to various kinds of childhood problems. I propose here that cognitive theory and cognitive therapy are unquestionably applicable to children, and I advocate a theoretical and practical model for change based on a self-control paradigm. This part of the book presents guidelines for assessment and evaluation of children's cognitive needs and deficiencies using self-control techniques, utilising both the child's developmental stage and specific behaviour problem as indices.

Chapters 11 and 12 emphasise the rationale for self-control therapy with children. Chapter 11 presents children's development in view of cognitive theory in general and the self-control model in particular, and in light of its relevance to childhood development. The chapter focuses on the natural acquisition of cognitive skills as part of children's development and the view of children's disorders as directly linked to deficiencies in cognitive skills. Chapter 12 presents the link between self-control and childhood disorders, emphasising the efficacy of self-control intervention with children. Chapter 13 presents Rosenbaum's (1990, 1993, in press) cognitive theoretical model comprising three self-control types and its adaptation to children. This chapter constitutes an attempt to propose a comprehensive theory for explaining children's behaviour, and to present a consistent intervention that includes both assessment and therapy. Chapter 14 describes my practical intervention model for imparting self-control skills to children, with an emphasis on case examples for applying the model to different childhood disorders such as enuresis, fears, and trauma and for achieving generalisation.

11

CHILD DEVELOPMENT AS A LEARNING PROCESS

THE DEVELOPMENT OF SELF-REINFORCEMENT

Behaviour theory explains children's development as shifts (a) from receiving reinforcement from others to being able to self-reinforce and (b) from the ability to enjoy real, concrete reinforcement to the ability to enjoy symbolic reinforcement. Infants are dependent on their parents or nurturing figures to control their behaviour and supply them with their basic needs such as food, clothing, and warmth. When parents approach their infants to feed them (i.e., give them concrete reinforcement), they also talk to, smile, and hug their infants. Shortly, even small babies who are only a few weeks old learn to cry in demand of a parent's presence, not only when hungry, but also as a means of receiving attention. In other words, these infants have already learned to enjoy symbolic reinforcement.

Table 7 presents the shift from real reinforcement to symbolic reinforcement, and from the need to receive reinforcement from others to the ability for self-reinforcement.

Symbolic reinforcements become more important and take on a more central role in children's lives as they grow older and begin to interact more with their environment. At that point, the need for social approval, to be accepted and appreciated by others, emphasises the role of symbolic reinforcement from others.

Table 7: The reinforcement matrix

	Reinforcement from others	Self-reinforcement
Real reinforcement	Infant receives food from parents	Buy oneself a present
Symbolic reinforcement	Smile, hug, compliment	Self-compliment

DEVELOPMENT AS AN OUTCOME OF OBSERVING AND IMITATING THE PARENTAL MODEL

Children's ability to control themselves is learned from being controlled by their parents, from observing the parents' way of behaving, and/or from being directly trained by parents through the use of reinforcement and punishment. For example, if a young boy touches the television set and his parents say 'no', the child understands that the parents do not want him to do that. In order to make his parents happy or to prevent being punished, the child will gradually learn to approach the television without touching it and may even imitate the parents' forbidding gesture or will say 'no' aloud to himself. Young children may practise this but be unable to refrain from the enticing act of touching the television unless the parents are physically present to intervene. Gradually, children internalise the parents' prohibition and try to obey.

As they grow older, children may be given an explanation such as: 'You're not supposed to touch it because you might break it.' At this point, being able to understand the reason as well as wishing to obey the parents (i.e., to receive reinforcement or prevent punishment) may enable children to avoid touching the television even when the parents are not present. Children's cognitive learning at this stage is already based on the ability to observe the situation, evaluate it, and make a decision, even without the parents' direct involvement. Understanding the concepts of good and bad allows children to compliment themselves (give themselves a symbolic reinforcement), saying: 'I'm a good boy. I didn't touch the television.'

.... desired behaviour, therefore, is an outcome of the ability to shift control from the parents (who forbid touching) to the child ('I shouldn't do it'), using self-talk, reasoning, and the understanding of concepts ('If I touch it, I may break it'). This shift helps children to develop appropriate expectations for the future ('I know I can choose the right behaviour') and contributes to the development of a sense of capability and competence ('I am a good boy. I know how I should behave and I can do it').

DEVELOPING EXPECTANCIES AND SELF-EFFICACY

The role of expectancies for human development and functioning are the cornerstones of Bandura's (1969, 1977) notion of self-efficacy. A child, in the first stages of walking, stops suddenly as she reaches a staircase, remembering falling down the day before and reasoning to herself, 'I can't make it. I'm afraid'. Before expectancies played a role in the child's behaviour, she did not avoid dangerous actions. Children need to be able to rationalise ('this is dangerous') in order to avoid specific actions. Bandura focused on the role of expectancies based on past experiences and of expectancies for future results as the primary mediators in developing a sense of competence among children, what he called 'self-efficacy' ('my belief that I can do it'). For Bandura, self-efficacy was a central notion because people who believe they can, try; and those who do not believe, quit. Self-efficacy encompass a main feature in children's ways of thinking and therefore, influence children's development.

THE ROLE OF AUTOMATIC THOUGHT IN CHILD DEVELOPMENT

Beck's cognitive theory (Beck, Rush, Shaw, & Emery, 1979) views child development as a process where the basic schemata composed of the child's experiences, assumptions, and attitudes towards the world are generated. Thus, a child who receives positive reinforcements from parents will develop a primary personal repertoire founded on the basic belief that 'I am being loved, I am good, I can succeed'. Such a child is likely to have positive automatic thoughts that will help him or her to generate positive attitudes and to adjust well to the environment. On the other hand, a child who receives constant criticism and is punished for much of his or her behaviour is liable to develop distorted thinking such as 'I am not good enough. I have to be the best, otherwise people will not like me'. As a result of such negative automatic thoughts, 'all or nothing thinking' may emerge. This frequent phenomenon among children usually entails a feeling of constant stress and pressure to be the best and to improve all the time, or else a feeling of helplessness, giving up, and believing that 'If I'm not good enough, there's no reason for me to even try'.

Children's basic schemata begin to evolve from the first years of life. Their early personal repertoire of schemata and core ideas reflects the outcome of their automatic thoughts and belief systems which will continue to influence their adult lives. The following two examples demonstrate Beck's concepts:

Parents of a 3-year-old girl described their daughter as follows: 'She doesn't act like a child. Rather, you'd think she was an old woman. She's so weighed down by her own thinking, that you would think she carries the weight of the whole world on her shoulders. And you know what? She was like that from the minute she was born.' From her early days, this young girl felt a constant need to make decisions, clarify events with her parents, and be involved in all the social, economic, and other aspects of her family life. By toddler age, she had already started developing her belief that the world was a difficult place in which to live. This pattern continued into adolescence, disturbing her enjoyment of peer interactions.

In another intake interview, with parents of a 16-year-old girl suffering from test anxiety, the parents described her as being too much of a perfectionist, always receiving the best grade and always working more than needed. The father said, 'She was always so good at everything. Even as a 4-year-old, when she used to paint in kindergarten, every picture took her hours to complete because she wouldn't get paint outside the lines, and she would choose her colours very carefully.' Looking back at Beck's notions, one can easily recognise the basic core idea that influenced her life at the age of 4 and continued to trouble her as a teenager: 'One must do the best and be the best. Not being the best means failure.' This idea was reflected in her perfectionism, in her staunch efforts to succeed, and in her fear of failure. Her belief system stated that 'If I'm not the best, then I'm useless' and that 'I couldn't live with myself as a failure and the world wouldn't like me then'.

An 'all or nothing' way of thinking can easily be seen in school-children who tend to be good students in subjects where they like the teacher and feel good, but tend to fail in subjects where they do not believe they are good enough. Again, the role of expectancies and automatic thoughts is very clear. Figure 1, containing what I term 'the "good" and "bad" cycles' can be very helpful when explaining these tendencies to children.

The identification of automatic thoughts among children is important in clarifying the main influences in a child's development in order to facilitate assessment as well as the selection of the treatment mode. Children view automatic thoughts as factual evidence ('I know I can't because I can't'), and also demonstrate a difficulty in separating thoughts, emotions, and behaviours. Asking young children what they are thinking may provide an answer such as, 'I'm afraid. I'm crying'; while asking them what they feel may elicit the response that 'this is frightening'. Usually, cognitive therapists do not focus on automatic thoughts due to the notion's difficulty for children to understand. The use of familiar examples and metaphors (see Chapter 3) can foster an explanation of this notion to children, helping them to change automatic thoughts to

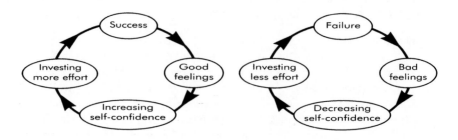

Figure 1: The 'good' and 'bad' cycles.

mediated ones, and to differentiate between evidence and impressions or between thoughts, emotions, and behaviours.

GUIDELINES FOR THERAPISTS ON IMPORTANT VARIABLES RELATING TO THE CHILD'S FUNCTIONING

The following guidelines help pinpoint important variables influencing the way the child functions. Therefore, before designing cognitive developmental therapy for a child, the therapist should attempt to singularise it:

- What kind of reinforcements are important and effective for this specific child?
- In what way does the child imitate, or is he or she influenced by the parents' behaviour?
- Can you identify basic points that lead to the way the child thinks of himself or herself (i.e., identify the child's self-efficacy; e.g., the child always believes it is possible to do so, or the opposite . . .)?
- What are the child's expectancies and automatic thoughts in relation to the presented problem?

SUMMARY

An important implication for cognitive therapy from the above review is the need to evaluate the child's developmental stage, features of the child's upbringing and education by his or her parents, and the parents' ability for self-control and for educating children for self-control. Much of children's distorted thinking derives from the parents, and many behaviours are an imitation of parental figures. It is difficult to change the child's way of thinking without helping the parents to understand the importance of this change as well as the need to expose children to positive thinking and positive reinforcement.

12

CHILD DEVELOPMENT AS AN OUTCOME OF SELF-CONTROL SKILL ACQUISITION

In childrearing and education, self-control comprises a main target. Self-control is a process occurring when, in the relative absence of immediate external constraints, a person engages in modes of behaviour that had previously been less probable than alternative available modes of behaviour (Thoresen & Mahoney, 1974). Self-control is called into play when new modes of behaviour need to be learned, when choices need to be made, or when habitual response sequences are interrupted or prove ineffective. Self-control, therefore, can be perceived both as a target in child therapy and also as the cause of many forms of problematic behaviour. Imparting children with self-control skills is a process that is learned and developed through children's interactions and relationships with their environment as they grow.

Two important steps can be pinpointed in a child's development of self-control. On the one hand, the adult control of children's behaviour (as described in the previous chapter) provides a model for the importance of control in obeying rules and norms; and, on the other hand, the development of verbal skills enables children to start controlling their own behaviour.

THE ROLE OF LANGUAGE IN CHILD DEVELOPMENT

Language has an important role for developing self-control skills. Luria (1961) described control of behaviour as shifting from being directed by others' talk to the development of self-talk aloud, and then finally to the capacity for silent self-talk. Mischel (1973) considered the evolution of self-control as resulting in the ability to inhibit impulsive responses. While language serves as an important mediating feature in the natural acquisition of self-control, it should also be considered as an important feature in verbal therapy—imparting and facilitating self-control skills, teaching the use of self-instructions, and helping the ability to change automatic-negative thoughts, etc.

The role of language implies, therefore, that cognitive child therapy should identify both (a) the child's verbal skills and the kind of words the child regularly uses (e.g., does the child often say: 'I can't! It's impossible!'?) and (b) the kind of language that parents use and ask their child to use in their communication (e.g., 'Only stupid children fail these kind of tests. You are smart! You will succeed'). Recognising the child's internal talk helps the therapist to identify the child's need for change. Kendall and Braswell (1985), for example, emphasised that impulsive children act without thinking—in other words, they do not use internal (mediated) talk to direct their actions but rather allow automatic thoughts to direct them.

THE LINK BETWEEN COGNITIVE DEFICIENCIES (SELF-CONTROI SKILLS) AND CHILDREN'S DISORDERS

As described in Part I of the book, self-control theory can provide an explanation for some of the childhood characteristics and disorders. The high frequency of childhood disorders in the population can be attributed to a lack of self-control skills, and this could also constitute the source of the familial link. Children acquire self-control skills by using their parents as role models, or by direct learning from them. Parents lacking in self-control skills tend to raise children who have a low ability to control themselves,

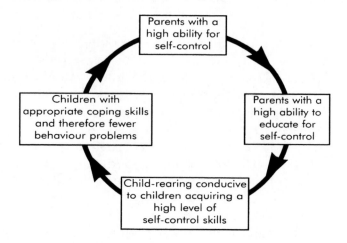

Figure 2:   The parent–child self-control loop.

which can develop into behaviour disorders (Ronen & Wozner, 1995). This cycle could be illustrated as shown in Figure 2.

In addition, as mentioned before, the higher percentage of spontaneous recovery could be understood in terms of the natural gain in self-control skills evident during maturation which may enable children, even without therapy, to solve their problems themselves. Boys mature more slowly and exhibit lower self-control skills than do girls (Kendall & Braswell, 1985; Rosenbaum, 1990), possibly accounting in part for the higher percentage of behaviour problems among boys. The high regression rate following behavioural interventions may be due to their lack of attention to the children's cognitive deficiencies; therefore, such treatments may help to temporarily eliminate disorders, but in the long run, without addressing the inadequate skills, a high probability of relapse exists. The acquisition of self-control skills through therapy may also clearly reveal the 'internal' cause of change as reported by parents and children—the modification of one's belief system and the feelings of empowerment that facilitate children's attempts to overcome their difficulties.

I was attracted to the area of cognitive therapy when, in the course of interviews with hundreds of children and parents

immediately after they had concluded successful treatment processes, I discovered a common denominator in many families regardless of the use of different therapeutic modes (e.g., whether
dynamic, behavioural, or Adlerian). Parents would report: 'Suddenly, my son seemed to have made a decision to take the treatment seriously, and from then on, he did!' or 'I saw that it was
really up to my daughter—when she was ready, she started tack-
ling the problem.' The children themselves would say: 'At that
moment, I felt I could overcome my problem. I started to believe in
myself.' Whether the significant factor was attributed to the child's
belief system, self-efficacy, motivation, or inherited self-control
skills, it was evident that some internal cause, something 'inside'
the child, was involved in the process of change, and was at least as
important as the technique being used.

Yet different cognitive dysfunctions require different cognitive
techniques that are devised to meet the specific needs of each child.
Technique selection will be determined by the treatment goal, such
as to decrease a behaviour, increase a behaviour, acquire new
skills, stop avoidance, or facilitate developmental functioning.

Empirical behavioural assessment looks at a characteristic pattern of behaviour and suggests classification of child disturbance
according to 'undercontrolled' versus 'overcontrolled' behaviours
(Mash & Terdal, 1988). Undercontrolled children, who evidence
aggressiveness, delinquency, hyperactivity, or impulsiveness, are
characterised by a lack of self-control skills and an impulsive manner of thinking and acting. Such children demonstrate difficulties
in tolerating frustration, delaying gratification, keeping attention
on target, or using problem-solving skills. Kendall (1993) suggested that impulsive children act without thinking or planning
and lack careful information processing in situations in which
thinking would be beneficial.

Overcontrolled children, who demonstrate fears, anxiety,
phobias, depression, and somatic complaints, are characterised by
avoidance behaviour caused by their fear of new and unknown
experiences. These children often overemphasise self-evaluation,
frequently setting themselves goals or criteria that are too high and
thereby under-appreciating their own achievements. Kendall
(1993) suggested that such children are limited to distorted thinking, where they misconstrue and misconceive social situations.

Achenbach (1993) reported that children with internalising problems benefit less from cognitive therapy than do children with externalising difficulties.

Not only do adults referring children to therapy (i.e., parents, teachers, counsellors) tend to be more aware of externalising or undercontrolled problems that disturb the environment (Hodges, Gordon, & Lennon, 1990), but also it seems that much more knowledge exists concerning the application of cognitive therapy to undercontrolled than to overcontrolled behaviour in children. The majority of studies included in Durlak, Fuhrman, and Lampman's (1991) meta-analysis and in Kendall's (1993) review were related to externalising problems.

In sum, the issues discussed in this section imply that the question facing mental health professionals today is not 'Is it possible to apply cognitive therapy to young and/or to internalising children?' but rather 'What knowledge do we need to adapt cognitive therapy to young and/or to internalising children?' or 'What modifications should be made in applying cognitive therapy to different problems in children?'.

GUIDELINES FOR THERAPISTS: ASSESSING CHILDREN'S SELF-CONTROL SKILLS

In assessing the child's self-control characteristics, the following guidelines should be helpful:

- Does the child use internal talk to guide behaviour?
- What kind of internal talk does the child use?
- Does the child seem able to apply self-control or does the child lack the necessary skills?
- Does the child's problem reflect an 'undercontrolled' or an 'overcontrolled' behaviour?
- Can you identify the parents' role in developing self-control skills? Do they present positive models for self-control?
- Can you identify the child's automatic thoughts? What implications do they have for the child's treatment?
- Can you see a connection between the child's verbalisations and way of thinking?

- Can you identify the link between what the child tells himself or herself and how the child feels?
- Can you see the link between the child's feelings and the child's behaviour?
- Is there 'all or nothing' thinking?
- Can the child reinforce himself or herself, or does he or she seem consistently to inflict self-punishment?

SUMMARY

Cognitive as well as behavioural treatments view children's behaviour as an outcome of learning processes. Behavioural conditioning (classical, operant, and imitation methods) and cognitive learning (development of self-talk, automatic thoughts, expectancies, and self-efficacy) have a major influence on the child's functioning. Therefore, therapy should target changes in all these domains, supervising parents in how to use behavioural methods (reinforcement, punishment, being model figures) for changing the child's behaviour and at the same time directly teaching the child in individual therapy how to change thoughts, deal with emotions, and modify behaviours. Self-control comprises a primary target in therapy; therefore, many educational and therapeutic programmes view the acquisition of self-control as an important step towards changing the child's functioning.

13

IMPARTING SELF-CONTROL TO CHILDREN

Self-control therapy has been applied to a range of different disorders such as impulsivity and hyperactivity (Kendall & Braswell, 1985; Kendall & Wilcox, 1980; Meichenbaum & Goodman, 1971); aggression (Kazdin, Esvelt-Dawson, French, & Unis, 1987); disobedience and disruptiveness problems (Copeland, 1982; Gross & Drabman, 1982); depression (Reynolds & Coats, 1986); and fears and anxieties (Barrios & Harmann, 1985; Graziano, Mooney, Hurber, & Ignasiak, 1979). However, this survey of self-control research reveals that even self-control treatments as reported in the literature, like other applications of cognitive therapy, have addressed conduct disorders more than emotional disorders. The targets of self-control interventions have included interpersonal thinking, means–end thinking, planning and anticipating skills, self-instruction, coping with stress, inhibiting responses, self-reinforcement, and use of problem-solving methods (Brigham, Hopper, Hill, Aramas, & Newsom, 1985; Cowen, 1980; Elias et al., 1986). The present chapter will describe the way to adapt self-control theory to children both for assessment and for therapy.

THE SELF-CONTROL THEORETICAL MODEL AND ITS ADAPTATION TO CHILDREN

Rosenbaum (1990, 1993) developed a theoretical model of self-control for adults that conceptualised three types of self-control:

Table 8:   Three types of self-control

Redressive	Reformative	Experiential
Keep current behaviour on target	Change current habits	Facilitate the generation of new behaviours
Reduce interferences with target behaviour	Interfere with current behaviour and replace it with a new behaviour	Reduce interferences with current emotional experiences
Achieve homeostasis	Achieve heterostasis	Achieve heterostasis: enrich personality repertoires
Stress reduction	Prevent future stress	Focus on immediate experience, expose to new and unknown experiences
Emotion and thought regulation	Emotion and thought regulation	Reduce cognitive control, be in tune with feelings
Reduce anxiety, pain, disturbing thoughts, poor mood	Delay of immediate gratification, planning, adherence to healthy behaviours, problem solving	Let go of analytical thinking, create images, be aware of sensations, be absorbed in current experiences

Source: Ronen (1995). © 1995 Springer Publishing Company, Inc., New York 10012. Used by permission.

redressive, reformative, and experiential. Table 8 presents a schematic representation of this model.

Redressive self-control focuses on the corrective function of the self-regulatory process. In response to a disruption of an ongoing automatic behaviour, the self-regulation process strives to achieve 'homeostasis' by keeping current behaviour on target (Rosenbaum, 1990). The individual aims his or her self-control behaviour towards reducing stress, pain, and disturbing emotions. Through regulation, the effects of the disruption on the smooth execution of routinised actions are minimised. For example, the increase of stress during an academic examination may prevent an individual from completing the assignment in his or her habitual manner. In this case, the treatment should focus on helping reduce anxiety and learning how to keep work on target without disturbance. Cognitive methods for redressive self-control include self-talk, relaxation, and imagination methods.

In *reformative* self-control the individual's efforts focus on changing his or her customary way of functioning (i.e., habits, lifestyle) and adopting a new behaviour. For example, for the person who is used to memorising the needed material while preparing for a test, reformative self-control will enable a change and improvement in learning, with a focus on understanding, planning, summarising, and evaluating material instead of merely relying on memory. Reformative self-control often includes the need to resist temptation and/or delay immediate gratification (Kanfer, 1977). While redressive self-control refers to the present, its reformative counterpart is directed towards achieving 'heterostasis' and towards preventing future stress and illness (Rosenbaum, 1990, 1993). Reformative methods include planning, adherence to healthy behaviours, and problem solving (i.e., defining a problem, generating alternative solutions, evaluating the alternatives, and implementing the solutions).

Experiential self-control (Rosenbaum, 1993) relates to emotions (Safran & Segal, 1990) and to the opening up of oneself to new experiences (Mahoney, 1990). Rosenbaum defined experiential self-control as individuals' ability to be sensitive and aware of their feelings and of specific environmental stimuli when cognitive control processes are temporarily relinquished. Experiential self-control is intended to facilitate the generation of new behaviours, to reduce interferences with current emotional experiences, and to achieve heterostasis, thus enriching the personality repertoire. Rosenbaum (1993) emphasised the benefits of being exposed to new and unknown experiences, reducing cognitive control, and letting go of analytic thinking from time to time. People employ experiential self-control when they face difficulties in becoming fully engrossed in experiences such as relaxation, hypnosis, meditation, listening to music, or enjoying social gatherings or a sexual relationship.

ADAPTING THE THREE-TYPE MODEL TO CHILDREN

Table 9 presents the extension and adaptation to children of Rosenbaum's model for self-control types, including children's targeted behavioural classification and problem behaviours linked to each self-control type, as well as treatment settings, techniques, and methods relating to the unique needs and features of childhood therapy: the objectives, training targets, targeted time frame, characteristic settings for the referred problem, and the kind of referred problem, in trying to help make the decision, 'What kind of self-control intervention is best for a specific child?'

Meta-analyses on the effectiveness of cognitive therapy with children have addressed the following kinds of problems: aggressive behaviour (Fleming, 1982; Forman, 1980); disruptive behaviour (Coats, 1979); oppositional defiant disorders (Lapouse & Monk, 1958); attention deficit disorders (Brown, Broden, Wynne, Schlesser, & Clingerman, 1986); impulsiveness (Kendall & Finch, 1979); hyperactivity (Kendall & Braswell, 1985; Kendall & Wilcox, 1980); emotional disturbance (Finch, Wilkinson, Nelson, & Montgomery, 1975); and social skills deficits (Gorton, 1985; Gresham & Nagle, 1980).

These behaviour problems within the realm of redressive self-control can easily be observed, identified, and translated into concrete concepts that are simple for children to understand. The necessary self-control intervention techniques (e.g., self-instruction, imagination, etc.) can easily be practised by children who, naturally at an early age, usually acquire such coping skills as talking to oneself, using imaginative play, and spontaneously finding methods to relax. Previous research has demonstrated that these redressive self-control techniques are successful in teaching children to overcome difficulties. Self-talk has been used to reduce stressful situations (Meichenbaum, 1985), pain (Karoly & Jensen, 1987), and impulsiveness and hyperactivity (Kendall & Braswell, 1985). Relaxation techniques have been used to decrease test anxiety and stuttering (Wolpe, 1982) and disruptive classroom behaviour (Hughes, 1988). The suggested techniques can be employed with children as young as 5 or 6 years who have a low cognitive level (at the concrete operational stage). The redressive self-control components can be taught and maintained through

Table 9: The adaptation to children of the three types of self-control

	Redressive	Reformative	Experiential
Aim	To solve existing problems, decrease disruptions	To change lifestyle, improve coping	Opening up to experiences
Target	Homeostasis	Heterostasis	Heterostasis
Time	Present	Future	Present, future
Problem's setting	Environment	Person (child)	Person (child)
Targeted behavioural classification	Under-controlled externalising	Overcontrolled internalising	Overcontrolled internalising
Child behaviour problems	Aggression Anger Conduct disorders Delinquency Disruptiveness Fears Hostility Hyperactivity Phobias Sociopathy Stress	Anxiety Apathy Depression Impulsivity Inhibitions Sensitivity Shyness Submissiveness Withdrawal	Anxiety Avoidance Depression Mental retardation Shyness Special education Withdrawal
Treatment setting	Therapy, educational	Therapy, educational, practice in natural environment	Primarily natural environment
Techniques	Self-instruction Imagination Relaxation	Criteria establishment Relaxation Problem solving Resisting temptation	Exposure to new experiences Relaxation Exposure to music, etc.
Methods	Modelling Role playing Rehearsal Record taking Discussions Written manuals	Homework assignments Practise exercises	Exposure to hobbies, youth groups, art, music, etc.
Age	5 years and upwards	11 years and upwards	3-4 years and upwards

modelling, role playing, behavioural rehearsal, and written manuals (Ronen, 1992, 1996b).

Much more problematic for children than redressive self-control
is the second type, reformative self-control, which is directed towards overcontrolled children with behaviour problems such as
withdrawal, depression, anxiety, etc. Anxious children have been
taught how to alleviate their fear of darkness (Kanfer, Karoly, &
Newman, 1975) and to use imagery to decrease test anxiety
(Hughes, 1988). However, most reformative self-control interventions do not facilitate overcoming or coping with a problem in the
present but rather focus on improving future functioning and
changing lifestyles. This goal of reformative self-control is more
difficult for children to achieve, in view of their limited perception
of time. It is difficult to motivate a young child to work on future
goals that are neither obvious nor concrete and have an outcome
that is not easily observed. In addition, the predominant cause for
children's referrals remains that of trying to alleviate difficulties
and return to homeostasis. Only a small proportion of children's
referrals will be explicitly aimed towards training in the generally
needed skills of resisting temptation, delaying gratification, or improving their lives.

Reformative self-control can also be beneficial for externalising
children whose basic needs are well met by redressive self-control
methods but for whom reformative techniques may help them to
cope better with resisting temptation and delaying gratification.
Many children who present undercontrolled behaviour also suffer
from a lack of reformative skills and would appreciate learning
these skills as part of overcoming a specific difficulty. They need to
acquire competencies such as withstanding temptation, learning to
plan, and using problem-solving skills. However, only very rarely
would these children be referred to therapy solely because of these
deficiencies or due to a wish to help the children change their
lifestyle or target heterostasis.

Although reformative treatments are less frequent among children (and especially among young children), this does not imply
that children do not suffer from these kinds of problem, but rather
that reformative self-control difficulties are more difficult to evaluate and parents are not always aware of their children's needs in
this area. Spivack and Shure (1974) stated that this kind of problem

stems from deficits in the interpersonal cognitive problem-solving skills that are essential components of sound adjustment throughout the lifespan. These skills include means–end thinking, problem solving, planning, establishing targets and criteria for evaluation, and adopting self-efficacious thoughts. Effective outcomes have been found in treating problems such as shyness (Harris & Brown, 1982), anxiety (Kanfer et al., 1975), and depression (Kingsley, 1987).

Experiential self-control is difficult to teach and apply in the case of adults. It operates differently with children, who seem better able to adjust to new environments, information, and people, and to be more open to new experiences. Childhood exposes children naturally to unfamiliar experiences in the form of learning or by meeting new friends at times of transition from one school to another. During normal development, children spontaneously use experiential self-control. One way of assessing children's problems relates to their readiness to expose themselves to new experiences. Overcontrolled children find it very difficult to leave a familiar environment and adapt themselves to new experiences. Rigidity in opening up to experiences such as a new class, a new teacher, new friends, foods, or clothes highlights deficiencies in children's adjustment (Mash & Terdal, 1988). Children who have special needs, such as those attending special education settings, usually find it difficult to adjust to changes in the classroom, to new classmates, teachers, or schedules. It is necessary for these children's well-being that they should be helped to experience these changes, especially if they have an exceptional difficulty in adjusting or letting go of control (such as always being well-mannered, clean, and quiet).

Openness to experiences is a skill that children should be intentionally taught by their parents and teachers from a very early stage. Helping the child avoid new stimuli may condition him or her to adhere rigidly to the same familiar foods, clothes, books, and games and to resent new ones. Parents can enjoyably teach experiential self-control by presenting the child with the benefit of music, dance, and the arts. Many parents send their children to extracurricular courses to develop specific skills such as additional languages, computers, etc. However, it is recommended that children be exposed not only to goal-directed knowledge acquisition but also to experiences that teach them to enjoy, relax, and find new areas of interest through drama, play, art, dance, and other classes that teach them to be in tune with their feelings. Imparting this skill will be different with children than with adults. It cannot be taught through rational explanations or verbalisations but rather through gradual exposure and training directed towards taking chances and risks, stepping out of the known environment and trying to enter a new one. These skills should be introduced as early as possible by kindergarten and school teachers, counsellors and parents, as well as by therapists.

CLINICAL USE OF THE MODEL

The adaptation of the three types of self-control outlined by Rosenbaum (1993) can comprise a helpful tool for clinicians in accommodating specific techniques to a child's particular needs. At times an integration of techniques deriving from the three types of self-control can best address different kinds of problem. For example, depressive children need to learn to interact with the environment, use self-reinforcement, use more realistic expectations and goals, and appreciate themselves more. These objectives imply a combination of reformative as well as experiential self-control. In contrast, anxious children need to expose themselves to frightening stimuli, identify internal cues for fear, learn to take records and evaluate themselves adequately, and mostly learn to reinforce themselves, indicating a combination of redressive and reformative self-control. Redressive and reformative self-control can both be seen as appropriate for impulsive, aggressive, and oppositional children who need to apply mediated thinking (Douglas, 1972), self-evaluation, self-talk, and planning (Kendall, 1993), as well as problem-solving models (Kazdin, 1988) that help the child predict outcomes and goals and improve self-esteem (Lochman, Burch, Curry, & Lampron, 1984).

Clinical utilisation of the model will be illustrated by three referrals to my clinic for the same problem in adolescents.

Three girls aged 16 to 18 years from three different schools were referred to therapy by their educational counsellors, due to test anxiety. All three of them seemed to be good students with good grades. As the dates for their secondary school matriculation examinations approached, these girls all started to develop behaviours such as stomach aches and headaches, vomiting, lack of sleep on the night before an examination, and feelings of anxiety during tests, with complaints of mental blocks, forgetting information, and writing nonsense. The assessments were conducted in light of the 3-type self-control model, in order to determine the nature of the specific problem and the most appropriate kind of treatment for each of the three girls. Test anxiety can be a response to different kinds of problem, personality characteristics, and needs, thereby necessitating different treatments.

The first girl, 'Betty', seemed to suffer from a redressive type of problem. She was a good student with good study habits, who was familiar with effective learning methods and did not present any other symptoms or anxieties. Her parents were very satisfied with the way she coped with her life in all areas other than this specific fear. Corresponding to the redressive method that pinpoints the need for the person to remove the disturbing feelings or behaviour in order to return to previous behaviour, it seemed as if the straightforward removal of Betty's anxiety during examinations would suffice for her to return to homeostasis and continue her day-to-day life. The importance of the examinations for her in relation to her aspiration to become a lawyer, necessitating very high grades, increased her anxiety. In her treatment with redressive self-control techniques, she learned to use relaxation, guided imagery, self-monitoring, self-evaluation, and self-reinforcement. After a short training period, she could cope better and continued studying and testing without fear.

Although the complaints of the second girl, 'Anat', were similar, careful assessment revealed a different pattern related directly to reformative self-control. Applying methods for anxiety reduction could not solve Anat's problem. Several days before an examination, Anat would not leave her chair for 8 to 12 hours at a time, studying very late without a break for food, sleep, or rest. She would learn the material by heart, trying to memorise every word mentioned in her books; therefore, forgetting one word would confuse her and prevent her from being able to answer the questions. Anat was evaluated as needing reformative self-control methods to improve her studying style by learning how to: plan her studying, work on rational criteria for success, decide on the amount of time and effort needed to put into learning, break studying into small units, and acquire effective study methods such as summarisation, differentiating important from trivial information, and comprehension rather than memorisation skills. In short, the treatment target was to improve her learning style and change her goals and expectations. A problem-solving model helped her to plan her learning and to study for fewer hours in a more effective manner.

Experiential self-control is exemplified by the referral of 'Debbie'. It was difficult to identify a specific disturbance in the assessment of Debbie's complaints. She seemed to exhibit a mastery of learning habits, and although she complained of anxiety, this also seemed within the normal response range for examination fears. Still, a noticeable decrease was evident in her grades and in her motivation and pleasure from learning. Soon, it became clear that Debbie's life had become centred around studies. Despite her social skills and history of having many friends and hobbies, she had neglected everything following her parents' request to concentrate on learning. While other teenagers were going out to parties, movies, ice skating, etc., Debbie would sit in her room studying. Soon, she became very depressed, lost her motivation, stopped smiling, and developed psychosomatic responses. Debbie clearly needed to enlarge her experiences. Her treatment was based on experiential self-control: The purpose of treating Debbie was to teach her how to bring back joy and happiness into her life, how to purposely let go of control and allow herself to take time out for other activities. She was encouraged to expose herself to enjoyable situations and to become more involved in leisure activities and spend less time on studying, although it might reduce her grades a little.

These three short case studies exemplify how to use the self-control types separately when designing interventions. However, often the same child needs an intervention that integrates all three types. The problem of encopresis may illustrate how the types may conflict yet complement one another if applied properly.

In cases such as encopresis, even when deficiencies exist in all three areas, it is recommended to begin with the redressive type (for removing the disturbance) and then progress to the other two. When an encopretic child suffers for a long time period, the problem may lie in inappropriate toilet habits and a problematic relationship with the parents which shifts attention to the child's soiling. However, the pain and danger associated with long durations of constipation and restraint necessitate that intervention begins using the redressive type of method. This will help the child remove the pain by stopping constipation. Only then is it possible to work on reformative needs by developing regular bowel habits. Although an increase in effective emptying habits constitutes the more important target, it takes longer to develop, requiring the establishment of new habits, enhancement of the child's awareness of internal stimuli, and muscle training. Experiential self-control would help the child shift his or her attention to more satisfactory experiences, learning to obtain parental attention through more enjoyable actions, and letting go of his or her wish to control the environment.

Another way to use the self-control model for children is by adapting the three types of technique to the child's developmental stage. Children with a high cognitive level are capable of using abstract methods, whereas children with a low socio-economic background or a low cognitive level need concrete methods (Copeland, 1982). In view of the higher skills needed for reformative methods, the therapist should first consider using redressive and experiential techniques for young children in low developmental stages and only later on should consider reformative interventions.

GUIDELINES FOR THERAPISTS IN ADAPTING THE THREE SELF-CONTROL TYPES TO CHILDREN

Look at the child's functioning and complaints and attempt the following:

- Can you identify redressive targets for intervention? What kind of techniques do you believe would help you work towards the identified behaviour?
- Can you identify reformative targets in the child's behaviour? Do these complement the redressive behaviours or are they completely different? What kind of techniques could help you in working towards the reformative targets?
- Can you identify some experiential targets? What kind of techniques could help you in changing these disorders?

SUMMARY

The three types of self-control—redressive, reformative, and experiential—could be either in competition with each other or complementary to one another. The role of the therapist is to identify the kind of disorder exhibited by the child, and while assessing the skill deficits and distortions, the therapist must design an intervention programme appropriate to the child's developmental stage, needs, and target behaviours. Children depend on adults for referral to therapy, and adults such as parents, teachers, or counsellors tend to be more attentive to externalising or under-controlled problems that disrupt the child's environment. Therefore, children are most often referred to therapy because of redressive kinds of problems. But, as therapists, we should be aware and sensitive enough to pinpoint reformative disorders and furthermore to identify even experiential deficits that pose a risk to the child's future. Therapeutic interventions with children include features from all three types of self-control as necessary to treat various aspects of children's disorders and needs.

14

SELF-CONTROL INTERVENTION MODEL AND CLINICAL APPLICATIONS WITH CHILDREN

In line with the aforementioned theoretical and empirical literature, I have developed an intervention model that consolidates the three types of self-control in order to modify children's externalising as well as internalising disorders. The model proposes an educational therapeutic process comprising five phases, as illustrated in Figure 3 (Ronen & Wozner, 1995). Each phase increases progress towards the achievement of control over the behaviour.

The five phases of the intervention model may be described as follows (Ronen & Wozner, 1995):

1. *Modification of maladaptive concepts.* The objective of the first phase is to teach the child that the disturbing problem is a behaviour that depends on him or her and that, therefore, can be changed if the child learns how to do so. Modification of misconceptions is achieved by redefinition and cognitive structuring. Socratic questions and paradoxical examples are used to help the child understand that the problem is not a matter of bad luck or illness, but rather is a function of motivation and will-power.

2. *Understanding the process of the problem.* To understand the process which evolved into the occurrence of the identified problem,

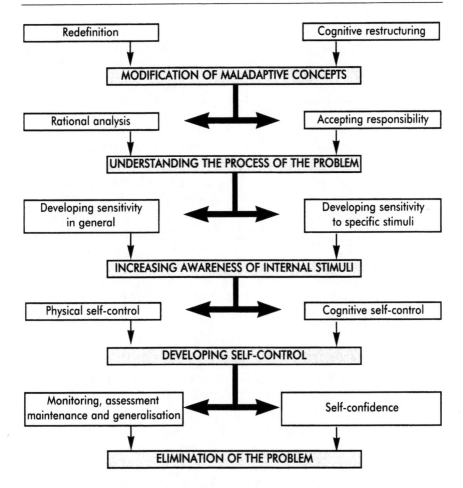

Figure 3: Five-phase intervention model. (Reproduced, with permission, from Ronen and Wozner (1995).)

the child is taught during the second phase about the connection between his or her brain, body, and final problematic behaviour. Treatment is accomplished here by rational analysis of the process and by helping the child to accept responsibility for its occurrence (Meichenbaum & Turk, 1987). Written materials, pictures of the human body, and verbal discussions are utilised.

3. *Increasing awareness of internal stimuli.* The third phase of the model is directed towards developing sensitivity in general and to

internal stimuli related to the specific problem in particular. Sensitivity is increased to stimuli in general (e.g., 'listening' to one's body, trying to concentrate on where and what one feels) and to the internal cues concerning the child's specific problem. Relaxation, concentration, and monitoring help to achieve these targets.

4. *Developing self-control.* The development of self-control skills is attained by teaching the child techniques for changing his or her automatic modes of behaviour to mediated ones. The child is trained in physical exercises (e.g., to continue running despite fatigue) as well as emotional exercises (e.g., to delay gratification). The techniques used include self-monitoring, self-evaluation, self-reinforcement, problem solving, and imagination.

5. *Elimination of the problem.* The problem is decreased by enhancing self-confidence and through monitoring, assessment, maintenance, and working towards generalisation. The fifth phase does not stand independently, but rather is achieved by using Kanfer's (1970) basic model.

Included in each of the five phases is a combination of three main components: learning, practising, and application. The *learning* component consists of teaching children concepts relating to their misconceptions; the processes involved in the occurrence of their problems; mediated and unmediated thinking; and techniques for changing behaviour. The *practising* component includes exercises that are performed in the intervention setting plus home assignments for additional experience. Practise is directed towards helping the child use different self-control techniques in different areas of his or her life, such as learning to identify his or her thoughts and emotional states, monitoring, recording, evaluating, and using self-talk and self-reinforcement. The *application* component integrates the newly acquired knowledge with the practised techniques in order to fully institute the process of changing the disturbed behaviour. Throughout the whole process of change, the child is perceived as a scientist whose target is to learn how he or she behaves and how to acquire knowledge in order to change. The role of the therapist is to be the child's supervisor, to suggest ways for practising and learning, and to direct the child in the self-help process.

OUTCOMES OF THE MODEL'S CLINICAL APPLICATIONS

Single-case design studies applying this self-control intervention model to children's problems such as sleep disorders (Ronen, 1993d) and encopresis (Ronen, 1993c) have demonstrated promising outcomes. A controlled study was also conducted using this model to treat a sample of 77 children aged 7½ to 12 years with nocturnal enuresis (Ronen, Wozner, & Rahav, 1992). In the enuresis study, the children were randomly assigned to one of four groups: bell and pad, token economy, self-control intervention, or a control set. The outcome revealed a similar success rate for each of the treatment modes. However, for the self-control group only, we found an immediate rate of decline in enuresis, a low dropout rate throughout the intervention, and a low relapse level in comparison with the bell and pad and token economy groups. The cognitive component clearly contributed to the long-term maintenance of improvement in behaviour. In another study aiming to assess the role of self-control on enuresis (Ronen, Rahav, & Wozner, 1995), the findings revealed a unique link between an increase in cognitive skills (i.e., self-control) and a decrease in bed-wetting.

The success of the intervention model pinpointed by these research studies—especially the long-term endurance of change and the children's ability to generalise their treatment gains to other areas of life—suggested the benefit these youngsters might have gleaned had they learned self-control as preventive skills. The original treatment model was therefore adapted into an educational programme (Ronen, 1994b), aiming to impart self-control methods to 312 second- and sixth-grade students as part of their regular school curricula, in comparison with a control group who did not study the programme. The educational programme was composed of two parts: (a) a 12-unit section incorporating self-control learning and training as well as practise of new knowledge, both at school and through homework assignments, and (b) a 7-unit section effecting the application of the learned material in the natural home environment and guiding the practise of each step in the full process of behaviour change. The study (Ronen, 1994b) showed that children who studied this model in school could 'self-change' behaviours such as disobedience and social problems. An increase was found in the children's self-control score as assessed both by children and by their teachers. Second-grade children succeeded more than did sixth graders, who did not work on the programme as seriously as their younger counterparts.

CLINICAL EXAMPLES

This section describes examples, taken from my private practice, for the use of the model. The names and some basic details have been changed in order to prevent identification of the cases.

Clinical Example 1:
Assessing and Treating Enuresis

A 10-year-old-boy, Ben, suffering from primary nocturnal enuresis with a frequency of six to seven nights each week, was referred to my clinic. Neither his parents nor his three younger brothers had suffered from enuresis; however, his uncle had wet his bed until the age of 13. The present intervention was Ben's third attempt to overcome his bed-wetting. At 7 years of age, he had tried to use a bell and pad but his parents complained that he never heard the bell. In addition, for a period of one year beginning at the age of 9, he was prescribed Tofranil, but the bed-wetting resumed when he stopped taking the medication.

Applying the five-stage assessment

Assessment stage 1: Who is the source of information? In order to obtain reliable information both on internal and external behaviours, the sources of information were the parents and the child. According to his parents and teachers, Ben was considered to be a very good student, to have many friends, and to get along well with his family. When asked about Ben's other problems, family members reported no major difficulties.

Assessment stage 2: Is the problem part of normal behaviour? Although enuresis is a normal behaviour for young children, the referred child should have overcome this behaviour and learned to control his bladder long ago. Wetting the bed at the age of 10 was deviant to the social norm, age norm, and developmental stage for this child; therefore, a clear need existed to teach the child to eliminate the enuresis.

Assessment stage 3: Does the child need therapy? Comparing the child's enuresis to social norms, age norms, and developmental stages pinpointed that Ben should have learned to control his bladder much earlier; to reiterate, the fact that the enuresis pattern had not markedly changed over recent years indicated that the problem was deviant and in need of intervention. The problem posed a risk to Ben's future, both socially, by preventing him from going away to camp or inviting friends to sleep over, and also emotionally, by creating a low sense of self-confidence which might influence other areas of his life. Changing the boy's bladder control would thus change his social and emotional functioning. The prognosis is very good for enuresis; a high percentage of recovery has been reported in the literature, and Ben evidenced high motivation for change. The fact that change had not occurred by this age indicated that the probability of spontaneous improvement without intervention was very low; therefore, the assessment pointed to the need for therapy.

Assessment stage 4: Choosing the setting for therapy. The question of who should be treated was easily solved by analysing the source of the problem. The parents seemed to function well with their son; they were able to challenge him and let him take responsibility for the change. Assessment highlighted the need to impart the child with lacking control skills. Therefore, the therapeutic setting was chosen to be individual treatment with Ben and to include occasional sessions with the parents in order to also foster their acquisition of knowledge and skills.

Assessment stage 5: Assessing the kind of self-control needed. Analysis of the child's self-control skills revealed that he lacked two kinds of skill: redressive and reformative. His main deficiency was in redressive self-control skills. Ben did not know how to control himself or how to change his sense of helplessness into a sense of resourcefulness. He needed to learn how to use self-talk and self-evaluation for improving his self-efficacy and to develop the ability to use mediating thoughts for controlling his bladder. Reformative self-control could contribute by establishing appropriate expectancies and planning long-term change.

The intervention procedure

Based on the five-stage assessment, Ben received an intervention consisting of a self-control model for changing his enuresis. The intervention, conducted at my private clinic, included the following phases: baseline, intervention, termination, and follow-up. The child and his parents visited the clinic once weekly for a 45-minute session throughout the intervention phase and once monthly through the follow-up phase.

The intervention phase, targeting Ben's enuresis, was conducted by the therapist and consisted of eleven 45-minute weekly sessions. The sessions dealt with self-control issues in accordance with the 5-stage intervention model described in the first section of this chapter. Each session utilised the following four procedures to apply the elements relevant to each stage of the intervention:

1. *The child's report.* The sessions began with Ben's report on the previous week. He presented his daily charts and notes with regard to the homework assignments he had completed, and discussions were held concerning the difficulties he had encountered that week. Emphasis was placed on his expressing feelings and thoughts regarding his progress.
2. *Curve constructions.* The therapist, with the child, next completed the progress curve according to the daily reports. On the basis of this curve, targets for the ensuing week were discussed.
3. *Presentation of a new theme.* After these tasks were completed, the therapist presented the child with a new issue for discussion (i.e., the next stage of the model or another aspect of the previous stage). The therapist explained the issue's significance and provided examples from Ben's everyday life to demonstrate. Ben was then asked to suggest an example of his own for the theme.

4. *Assigning homework.* Every session was conducted by giving Ben new homework assignments. The assignments included completing the daily chart and applying the new theme at home or in his school setting. The therapist and Ben discussed possible difficulties the child might be likely to confront, and ways to overcome them.

I shall now describe in more detail the application of the 5-stage self-control model to Ben's enuresis intervention phase:

Intervention stage 1: Modification of maladaptive concepts concerning enuresis. The objective of this stage was to teach the child (a) that enuresis is a behaviour that can be changed like other kinds of behaviour and (b) that change depends on the child. Ben's self-evaluations, where his predicted rate of progress could be compared to his actual rate of enuresis, reflected self-perceptions and self-efficacy. He saw enuresis as something beyond his control, something that occurred because 'it just escaped' or because he 'didn't feel it' or 'was sick'. Ben perceived himself as a helpless victim of superior forces. Modification of maladaptive conceptualisations was achieved by redefining the enuretic process as a behaviour which can be controlled and by cognitive restructuring of thoughts and concepts concerning personal beliefs. In this stage, use was made of Socratic questions and paradoxical examples to help Ben understand that bed-wetting does not depend on bad luck or illness but, rather, is a function of motivation and will-power.

The purpose of the following conversation was to change Ben's misconception relating to his belief that while asleep he could not feel anything and therefore could not control any night-time behaviour.

Therapist: What do you think, why do you wet your bed at night?
Ben: Because I don't feel anything when I sleep.
T: Let's check this out. How many times do you fall out of your bed?
B: Never.
T: How come? You do turn over in your bed while you're asleep, don't you?
B: When I get close to the edge of the bed I just turn to the other side.
T: Aha! Let's see something else. Did it ever happen during the winter that your blanket fell off?
B: Sure!

T: What did you do?

B: I woke up and covered myself.

T: You see, even while you are asleep there are things you feel. You feel the edge of the bed, you feel cold. Even while you are asleep, you feel certain things.

B: Right.

Intervention stage 2: Understanding the process of enuresis. The objective of the second stage was to teach the child about the process of bed-wetting and the connections between the bladder, the brain, and the final behaviour (emptying the bladder). Children are assumed to find it easier to change a behaviour when they understand how it is carried out and how it is affected by different actions.

In this stage, Ben learned about the process culminating in urination: how drinking fills the bladder and causes the unpleasant pressure that is transmitted to the brain, and how the brain then 'sends' commands to the valve to open and release the urine, an action which ends the unpleasant sensation. Information was taught about the brain, which is responsible for every one of our behaviours, and about the connection between the brain and the body. Ben learned the differences between automatic unmediated commands and mediated commands.

This stage was conducted through rational analysis of the process, using written materials and pictures of the human body, and through helping the child to accept responsibility for the process by learning to change the brain's command. Ben practised identifying automatic thoughts and using self-talk and self-recording to change unmediated thoughts into mediated ones. Various props were used, such as plastic bags to show how the bladder fills up, and drawings of the bladder and brain. Examples of other automatic responses which can be modified were introduced, and Ben was taught internal dialogues for instructing himself. He was challenged to identify other automatic thoughts he may have had (e.g., related to being disruptive in the classroom or to not doing homework) and to change them into mediated thoughts. Then Ben was asked to try to change the automatic response of bed-wetting into self-restraint or awakening.

Intervention stage 3: Increasing bladder control. The objective of the third stage was to increase the child's awareness of the bladder pressure and to increase the functional capacity of the bladder. Although internal stimuli are difficult to identify, they have at least as strong an influence on behaviour as the use of external stimuli (Bandura, 1969). Awareness of internal stimuli is an important step towards controlling one's own behaviour in that it helps in early identification of sensations, emotions, and behaviours (Bandura, 1969, 1977). Also, being aware of internal stimuli helps in changing unmediated processes into mediated ones (Kanfer & Philips, 1970; Miller, 1979).

A functional relationship exists between the size of the bladder and enuresis. A small bladder fills up quickly, and the signals it sends are less clear than those of a larger bladder (Fielding, 1980, 1982). In this stage, sensitivity to internal stimuli in general (e.g., the sensations of hunger, tiredness, etc.) and to the sensations of the bladder in particular, were increased. Ben was asked to report his sensations in general (e.g., heart beat, palpitations in the stomach, reception of noises, etc.) and bladder pressure in particular. Retention control exercises were practised by the child both to enlarge the bladder (Hallman, 1950) and to increase sensitivity to internal stimuli. He was asked to practise restraining urination during the day and to concentrate on the ensuing sensations. His parents were instructed to ask their son: 'Why are you going to the toilet?', 'What are you feeling?' and 'Where in the body is this sensation located?' Ben thus learned to identify the specific physical sensation occurring when he could not withhold any longer and must urinate.

Intervention stage 4: Developing self-control. The objective of the fourth stage was to teach the child self-control techniques for changing the unmediated behaviour into a mediated one, thereby eliminating the enuresis. This fourth stage was achieved by training Ben first to gain physical control and then to acquire control over emotions, thinking, and behaviour. The techniques learned included the use of self-monitoring and assessment, self-instruction and self-reinforcement, imagery, and problem-solving techniques. Practice included exercising self-control in day-to-day activities through home assignments (e.g., stopping talking when he wants to say something, stopping playing, or crying, or drinking when thirsty, or eating when hungry). Ben was instructed to continue the physical exercises even when he felt tired or experienced some other difficulty. He learned that as confidence grows the chances of success also increase.

The following example is taken from the fifth session with Ben. During the first four sessions, Ben learned to identify his misconceptions, understand the process of behaviour, and increase awareness of internal stimuli. At this point, Ben had already decreased his frequency of enuresis from 7 wet nights a week to 2–3 nights, and he even went on an overnight trip with his class. The aim of this session was to present Ben with techniques to be used for self-control.

Therapist: You have successfully decreased your wetting nights. Still, there are nights when you wet the bed. How do you explain this?
Ben: I can't stop myself from wetting the bed.
T: You say that you can't control yourself. Is this the case all of the time?
B: Yes.
T: Two weeks ago you went for a trip with your class, did you wet there?
B: Are you crazy? That would embarrass me terribly.
T: So what did you do?
B: I tried very hard and I succeeded.
T: Exactly! You see, when you think it's important for you, you can control yourself. Now, imagine that I promise that your parents will give you the dog you desire so badly if you do not wet the bed. Would you succeed in doing it?
B: Sure I would.
T: You see, whenever it's important for you, if you're either afraid of being punished (having your friends notice that you wet the bed) or if you wish to gain something (a dog), you put in more effort and succeed in staying dry. Doesn't that mean you can control your enuresis when it is important?
B: Maybe. I'm not sure.
T: How about us checking this out by you imagining every night for the next week that you will get that dog you want if you stay dry, and putting in as much effort as you can?
B: I'll try.

Intervention stage 5: Elimination of the enuresis: Maintaining and generalising the outcome. The fifth stage did not stand independently but, rather, was achieved by using self-recording, self-evaluation, and self-reinforcement throughout the whole process, thereby gradually increasing self-confidence. One of the main foci of this stage was relapse prevention. Regression often occurs because, as one regresses, one tends to lose confidence in the ability to control the situation, and then a chain of regression occurs (Marlatt & Parks, 1982). In this stage, Ben was cautioned to regard any case of bed-wetting as an incidental event rather than turning the disappointment from bed-wetting into despair, which could result in a decrease in efforts and more wet nights. To maintain the outcomes, he continued monitoring and reporting to the therapist while gradually stopping the retention control training, but maintaining his early bedtime and avoidance of drinking before bed. Eventually, Ben returned to his regular schedule and still maintained a positive outcome. Generalisation was fostered by having Ben try to apply self-control methods to other areas such as behaviour in the school setting, among friends, or within the family. Following-up sessions at 1, 2, and 4 months after termination approved of the child's success in managing his own self-change programme, and therefore, enable the conclusion that generalisation was truly achieved. No regression 4 months after termination indicate the possibility that the child has acquired skills he can apply and maintain.

Clinical Example 2:
Self-Control Exposure Therapy for Treating Fears and Anxieties

This example discusses ten Israeli children suffering from treatment refractory anxieties who responded with increased severity and new symptoms to the real threat of harm during the 1991 Gulf War. All of these children were referred to my private clinic by their parents during April 1991, four to six weeks after the end of the Gulf War. Like all of the citizens of Israel, in response to frequent night-time air-raid sirens, these children had awakened and moved with their families into air-raid shelters in their homes that had been sealed off from potential chemical attacks, where the children were fitted along with other family members into gas masks. They evidenced fear reactions such as a feeling of dryness in the mouth, asking many questions, listening closely to the radio, tension at nightfall, headaches, and difficulty falling asleep. However, unlike the other members of their families, the anxious behaviours of these children did not decrease after the war.

The reason for referral as presented by the parents was similar for all ten children: anxiety reactions and features of separation-anxiety disorders that continued following the war. All of the children evidenced sleep disorders such as difficulty falling asleep, frequent awakening during the night, resistance to staying in their own beds, entering the parents' bed, and nightmares (Ronen, 1996a). However, an accurate account of the children's past highlighted a history of previous anxieties from early childhood among all of the referred children: sleep terror disorders (i.e., refusal to sleep, forcing the parents to stay with them until they fell asleep, frequent awakening at night). All of the parents reported that their children had always been too anxious (e.g., 'He acts like an old woman').

Applying the five-stage assessment

Assessment stage 1: Who is the source of information? The assessment was based mainly on children's reports of their own feelings, due to the fact that parents are not a reliable source for assessing children's emotional disorders.

Assessment stage 2: Is the problem part of normal behaviour? Such fears and anxieties are behaviours deviant to the children's ages, social norms, and developmental stages, and they do not typify normal development.

Assessment stage 3: Does the child need therapy? The deviance of the problem in relation to all criteria (diagnostic criteria, age, developmental stage, and social norms) highlighted the importance of therapy. The risk to the children's future and their prognosis showed the need to treat the children. This need was accentuated concerning the avoidant aspect of the children's functioning, which hindered their participation in social activities and meetings with friends, at an age when social interactions are crucially important for children's normal adjustment (i.e., avoiding social activity posed a risk to the children's future well-being).

Assessment stage 4: Choosing the setting for therapy. Considering that the problem was mainly fears and avoidant behaviours, these children could be expected to find it difficult to face fearful situations. The chosen setting was therefore the family, with the parents serving as supervisors for the children's assignments. This setting also enabled intervention regarding a side effect of the referred problem: parents' tendency to reinforce their children's fears by comforting them and letting them remain in the parents' presence.

Assessment stage 5: Assessing the kind of self-control needed. The main skill these children lacked was the ability to let go of control, to be ready to experience new stimuli, and to open up to new situations; therefore, they were evaluated as needing experiential self-control. The treatment selected was self-control exposure therapy.

The intervention procedure

Like in the previous case example, the sessions dealt with self-control issues in accordance with the 5-stage intervention model described in the first section of this chapter. Each session utilised the same four procedures to apply the elements relevant to each stage of the intervention:

1. *The child's and parents' report.* The intervention was presented as a scientific task. Parents and children were asked to take part in a scientific project targeting change in their behaviour. The goal of self-observation was defined as learning how they behave and increasing awareness of internal stimuli (i.e., fears, somatic complaints in the children; the need to protect in the parents), in order to be able to 'self-change' them (Ronen & Wozner, 1995). Therefore, participants were asked to learn how to observe, and record their own behaviour. For example, they were asked to observe: (a) their need to urinate, including the pressure of the bladder and the sense of relaxation after emptying themselves; and (b) their response to an argument with other members of the family, what they felt, how they reacted, and so on.
2. *Curve constructions.* In order to present the children and the parents with the process of the fear reduction, the therapist used the daily record of the rate of fear and drew the fear-curve. On the basis of this curve, targets for the ensuing week were discussed.

3. *Presentation of a new theme.* After these tasks were completed, the therapist presented the child with a new issue for discussion such as the normal nature of fears, the way fear increased or decreased, the role of thoughts in eliciting fears.
4. *Assigning homework.* Every session was conducted by giving the children new exposure assignments. The assignments included completing the daily chart and applying the new theme at home or in the school setting, but, most of all, practising exposure *in vivo.*

The intervention was presented to participants as a combination of self-control methods for changing one's belief system and imparting exposure skills, together with self-guided exposure methods for a gradual decreasing of anxiety and fear consisting of the basic 5 stage model.

Intervention stage 1. Modification of maladaptive concepts. Children and parents learned that fear is a behaviour they have acquired and, therefore, it is up to them to change it. They learned to understand that, although difficult, it is possible to control fear and by that means, decrease it.

The target and process of treatment were presented in concepts appropriate for children's level of understanding.

Intervention stage 2. Understanding the way fears increase and maintain. By learning to fear specific stimuli, children have developed automatic thoughts of expecting the fear to increase and caused a 'fear of fear' situation, eliciting avoidant behaviour. Parents had learned to reinforce the misconception that 'fear is overcome by avoiding stimuli' by giving the child reassurance and reinforcement which increased the fear. Therefore, the process of intervention was presented as a process of learning a new habit (coping) for changing the old, maladaptive one (avoidance). The explanation was in simple, concrete words, with many examples taken from children's day-to-day life.

Intervention stage 3. Increasing awareness. Children learned to identify their internal stimuli concerning fear. They were asked to rate their fears on scale of 1 to 10 with 1 denoting 'I have no fears at all' and 10 denoting 'the fears are very high'. Before, during, and after exposure assignment children were asked to rate their fears, and try to identify what exactly they felt, in what part of their bodies (hurt bits, stomach aches, dryness in their mouth).

Intervention stage 4. Developing self-control. Parents and children were told about the importance of the daily exposure tasks as necessary to overcoming fears and anxieties. Explanations were presented in simple language appropriate for children, such as:

> There is something like a battle going on between you and the things you're afraid of. As long as you run away from your fears, they will follow you, trying to catch you. And by trying to keep away from your fears, they grow bigger and bigger. On the other hand, when you show those fears that you aren't afraid, by trying to stand still and face them, your fears become frightened, and *they* run away from *you*! And that's how you can get your fears to become smaller.

In preparation for exposure assignments, the children were asked to give examples of situations they feared in the past but of which they eventually stopped being afraid (e.g., swimming, going to the beach, riding in elevators, riding a bicycle). In each of the given examples, the therapist demonstrated how the children had overcome their fears by being exposed to the situation. Children were told that each time they perform a feared task for the first time it will be a bit difficult, but that if they don't give up, then the second time it will be easier. When it becomes very frightening, they can comfort themselves by saying: 'Well, it's worth while to go through this today, because it will make it easier tomorrow.' The children were told that their anxiety would decrease if they continued exposing themselves, and that the more they exposed themselves, the better they would progress.

The children themselves were placed in charge of selecting the individual kinds of exposure tasks, degree of exposure, and length of exposure. For example, one boy decided to begin with remaining alone in his bedroom at night with one of his parents near, but outside the room. He planned his exposure so that each day he increased the time he would stay alone and made a change in how close his parents were in the house and, eventually, outside the house. Parents were encouraged to support and comply with their child's decisions regarding the types and pace of exposure tasks. They were permitted to advise but not to decide for the child.

In order to help children initiate the exposure, the therapist presented a prediction 'game'. The children were asked to prepare a list of exposure tasks, and each of the parents was told to guess the answers to four questions:

1. Will your child be brave enough to expose himself or herself?
2. Will he or she need your help?
3. How frightened will he or she become?
4. How long will he or she be able to stay in the situation?

The children were challenged to win the game by proving to the parents that they could achieve more than the parents predicted. In turn, the parents were instructed to make their guesses feasible in order that the child would not be frustrated by failing to realise the parents' expectations.

Five methods were introduced and practised to help children face and cope with their fears: (a) using imagination ('Pretend you are Superman and nothing can scare you', or 'Imagine how good it will be once you can go everywhere without needing your parents to accompany you'); (b) self-reinforcement ('If I stay in this situation, I can get another token'); (c) positive self-talk ('I know I can do it'); (d) commands to the brain ('I will stop those automatic thoughts of fear and will command my brain to think of my success'); and (e) self-compliments ('I've succeeded! I believe I can continue!') (Ronen & Wozner, 1995).

Self-reinforcement and self-talk were practised both by parents and children, who had all been asked to compliment themselves for accomplishing the daily assignments. For example, children were taught to say: 'I'm great! I succeeded in exposing myself without running away.' Parents were taught to compliment themselves with statements such as: 'I'm a good parent! Although it's hard for me to face my child's difficulties in exposure, I did not prevent him from exposure! Well done!'

The parents were instructed to reinforce their children each day for any or all of three achievements: (a) anxiety predictions similar to reality; (b) completion of exposure assignments; and/or (c) a tendency towards decreased anxiety levels (or actually, as rated, increasing calmness) during exposure (see below) in comparison to previous days. The parents were also asked to compliment the child for his or her small steps towards success every day, both verbally and on the child's written daily record (e.g., 'Well done! You did great!'). Role playing was used to help parents who had difficulty giving their children compliments. Three kinds of reinforcement were used: (a) tokens given to the child for each success, which could be exchanged for gifts of personal preference (e.g., a compact disc, a book on computers); (b) individually selected social rewards as appreciation for progress (e.g., inviting friends to come over, going out with parents to see a movie); and (c) symbolic reinforcement, where parents were instructed to compliment their children every day for their efforts and for their progress.

Parents were told that a child's problem very easily becomes the centre of family life because of the parents' concern and desire to help their child overcome it. Very soon the child learns to enjoy the family's attention, which then serves as a secondary gain, helping to maintain and magnify the problem. The therapist reinforced the parents for 'being such good parents that you're ready to experience these difficulties of refusing your child's requests in order to really help him or her overcome the fears'. The results proved that all ten families reported a significant improvement in the anxiety behaviours demonstrated following the war. The most significant changes were in the children's ability to leave their homes, stay at home without parents, and attend school. Immediately after the first treatment session, the children who had completely avoided school since the war returned to school. During the following weeks all of the children learned to go to and from school alone, without a parental escort. Other changes noticed were activities with friends. During the intervention, all of the children started to take part in normal peer activities inside and outside the house. Four of the children went to their friends' homes but asked their parents to meet them if it was dark. Six of the children returned to attending afternoon extracurricular activities (such as basketball, chess, Judo) which forced them to leave home and go to where the activities were held.

Intervention stage 5. Elimination of the problem. As children improved and fears decreased, children and parents learned about the possibility of regression. They were told that regression sometimes occurs as a normal part of progress and that they should not give up, but rather should view regression as temporary and try to avoid turning a single regression into a chain of regressions.

The results of the intervention regarding post-war behaviours in comparison to the intake avoidance profile revealed a very noticeable change for each of the children. The most surprising outcomes of the exposure procedure were those relating to an improvement in the long-standing separation–anxiety behaviours evident prior to the war.

Clinical Example 3:
Teaching Generalisation by Helping Children to Help Themselves

As generalisation is not learned automatically, the self-control model could also be used for the purpose of consistently teaching children how to generalise treatment outcomes. The following example is of Dan, a 12-year-old boy who had been treated in order to eliminate his nocturnal enuresis and who selected nail biting as the target of self-change.

Nail-biting intervention

After the first six weeks of intervention for enuresis (using the same treatment as described in clinical example 1), I saw evidence of significant progress in Dan's ability to control his enuresis, and asked him to select another of his problems and treat himself by the same method that had been used to treat his enuresis. The child decided to choose the problem of nail biting. He was a habitual nail biter who used to damage his fingers to the point where they were painful and bleeding. Dan was asked to treat himself for the nail biting as he wished, but to maintain a daily record of what he chose to do. He was allowed the last five minutes of each session (while being treated for enuresis) to present his records to the therapist.

One week after this generalisation phase of his intervention was initiated, Dan reported that he had examined his nail-biting habits. He discovered that he bit his nails less in the evenings (in the presence of his parents) and more during the mornings (at school). He suggested that the most difficult time for him to avoid nail biting was the morning. Noticing these conclusions, Dan decided to divide his day into three parts (i.e., morning, afternoon, and evening), and he first focused his efforts on decreasing nail biting during the evenings. When he noticed a change, he put more effort towards the afternoons. The mornings were left to the end.

There was one thing he requested from the therapist: he said that he knew how to measure enuresis but had no idea how to measure changes in nail biting. I suggested that he rate his own efforts using a scale of 0–10, where 0 signalled no effort to stop biting, and 10 represented not biting at all. After receiving this minor assistance from me, Dan conducted the rest of his intervention independently.

In his self-intervention, Dan used self-verbalisations and self-reinforcement. He decided to spend his weekly allowance (pocket money he received from his parents) only if he progressed, and to return it to his parents if he regressed. His parents also reinforced him with symbolic reinforcement while noticing the change ('we are very proud', 'you really succeeded', 'you've grown up').

Termination

The criterion for termination of the primary intervention (for enuresis) consisted of 21 consecutive dry nights. In his last session, having achieved this criterion, Dan completed the Self-Control Scale and the two progress curves—i.e., one for enuresis and one for nail biting—and then a comparison of these to his baseline scales was discussed. Dan was requested to continue taking records for the next six months.

Follow-up

During the six-month follow-up period, Dan visited the clinic once a month and showed his records. At the last follow-up meeting, he once again completed the Self-Control Scale.

Results

With regard to his enuresis, a significant change in bed-wetting frequency was noticeable immediately following the first intervention session. The boy's progress was quite remarkable: in the eleventh week he already revealed full control of his bladder, an achievement which lasted through the follow-up period. During the first follow-up month, there were two accidents: the first on a night when he was very excited because he planned to sleep at a friend's house the next day for the first time, having never slept out because of his enuresis. The second was the night of Independence Day, when he went to a party, drank all night, and fell asleep at 5 a.m. He slept until 9 a.m. and woke up wet. After these events, he remained dry and never wet the bed for the remaining five months.

Figure 4 presents the progress curve for the intervention and follow-up periods. The comparison of his scores on the three administrations of the Self-Control Scale showed a striking change. His self-control score jumped from –15 prior to intervention, to 14 at the end of intervention, and to 17 at the end of the follow-up period. With regard to his nail biting, it took Dan six weeks to stop biting his nails. In the sixth week, he entered the clinic with long nails, insisting that he had wanted to wait to cut his nails until he had shown them to the therapist. During the follow-up period, the boy's fingers also recovered, providing the best proof of change.

Clinical Example 4:
Treating Traumatised Children Through Cognitive–Constructivist Therapy

I did not describe constructivist therapy as a separate section since, for me, constructivism in general is a part of cognitive therapy. With children in particular, constructivism is a necessary part of each intervention since, in any event, the most important part is the way the child views and construes the event rather than the reality. Therefore, the next example illustrates the use of cognitive–constructivist therapy with children in general and with traumatised children in particular.

Constructivism, as the theoretical framework for my model, emphasises the person as a scientist who actively learns to conduct his or her own life through the structuring of events, facts, and experiences (Kelly, 1955). Kelly suggested that people are participants and agents who do not merely react to the world, but rather act on

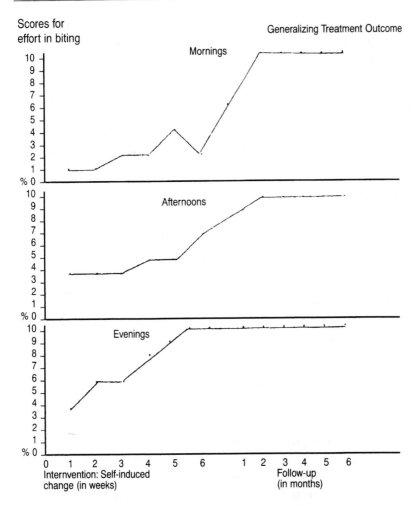

Figure 4: Self-treatment for nail-biting.

it. The person is seen as a builder or, as Kelly stated, as an 'architect' of his or her own schemata and realities. I propose that through self-control therapy, children may be imbued with the specific cognitive skills necessary to achieve these constructivist goals. Constructivist therapists enable this process to transpire by focusing on an attempt to understand (through their own construct systems) each traumatised child's individual and inner world, set of personal meanings, thinking style, and need for meaningful relationships.

Although an external event is by definition crucial to a traumatic experience, I believe that *the way children construe the event* accounts for the difference between one child who overcomes the trauma and continues to live as fully as before and another child who responds to the same traumatic event by developing symptoms and post-traumatic stress disorder. What differentiates these two responses to trauma is not the event itself but rather the way an individual child attributes meaning to the event, processes it, and reconstructs it. That people construct their own reality is more important than so-called 'objective' events (Mahoney, 1991), highlighting the important issue of how people's lives should be understood and lived (Rychlak, 1968). Constructivism, therefore, can be considered the most important feature in dealing with trauma. The trauma cannot be avoided or changed, but the way one processes it and deals with accompanying feelings of guilt, fear, and so on can have a critical impact on the ability to live a full and adaptive life following the traumatic experience.

The main focus of the model—as a cognitive–constructivist approach—is the perception of the child as a scientist (Kelly, 1955) who learns to formulate hypotheses about what will happen under certain conditions and then evaluate the hypotheses in light of the ensuing outcomes. In his or her role as scientist, the child uses self-recording, self-evaluating, and self-reinforcing techniques throughout the whole process of change. An emphasis on personal meaning-making exposes children to the processes through which they had constructed their personally relevant schemata, increasing awareness to the way each construct has served them and challenging them to reconstruct it in a more fulfilling and satisfactory way. The children thus learn to identify what happened to them and how they responded, to change the meaning, and to construct a new reality (Ronen, 1996b).

The intervention model is similar to the above presented model. However, because of the unique nature of trauma for children, every phase of the self-control model also targets three main aims, two dealing with the child's present behaviour and the third dealing with the future. The first aim targets the immediate experience of the trauma by helping the child to accept that a traumatic event was experienced; to become aware of and allow himself or herself to express the thoughts, emotions, and behaviours it elicited; and to try to live with these and to understand that in time these feelings could be changed. The second aim targets the attempt to change the meaning (i.e., the construction) of the event in order to cope with it more effectively. The third aim is directed towards the future, helping the child to grow out of the traumatic experience and empowering him or her to be open to the world and give other experiences a chance.

The proposed model comprises five phases. Each phase targets all three of the aims: facilitating the child's understanding and acceptance of his or her system of constructs regarding the event; helping the child to change the meaning of the situation (along with the concomitant beliefs, feelings, etc.); and challenging the child to be open to new experiences (Ronen, 1996b).

Phase 1: Modification of maladaptive concepts

In the first phase, the therapist tries to understand the child's own explanations and belief system concerning the traumatic event (i.e., aim 1). This phase endeavours to help the child to change the meaning of the traumatic event and to construct new meanings that will improve coping. Often evident at this time are children's sense of guilt or responsibility for the traumatic event, their lack of awareness regarding their problems, and their belief that their suffering will be unremitting. Like a tennis player—who meets the ball at a certain point and raises it up—the therapist should help the child articulate a reconstruction of the event, give it another meaning, and change his or her belief system (aim 2). In contrast with the possible denial and avoidance of adults in the child's environment, the therapist should reinforce the child's belief that the event did happen and that how he or she thought, felt, or behaved in response to that event also occurred.

The child's negative conception about the interminableness of these reactions must also be addressed; the child can be introduced to the alternative that, in time, those behaviours, thoughts, and feelings could be changed. A main target of this phase is to obtain the child's agreement to try working with the therapist, under the assumption that the response to the trauma is a behaviour and that a behaviour can be changed in certain circumstances. During this stage, the therapist can use cognitive restructuring, redefinition, metaphors, and imagination to demonstrate the accessibility of change. For example, the child's belief that 'I can't, I'll never be able to cope' can be modified to 'It's hard and I'm afraid, and I don't know how, but I will learn to overcome this'.

Consider another example. If a child was traumatised by his father beating him, the meaning of the event could be changed from 'I was a bad boy and I made Dad angry, so he beat me up' to 'It wasn't my fault; it didn't depend on anything I did; I wanted to be a good boy, but he didn't understand me and hit me.' By changing the child's negative conceptions regarding self-blame, a first step is being made towards helping him to stop avoidance and start exposure to new and other experiences (aim 3).

Phase 2: Understanding the process of the trauma experience and the child's response

Often children think that they are managing well and do not need help, but they exhibit behavioural disorders that convey the problems they are experiencing. Therefore, a need exists to increase the child's understanding of the relationship between the traumatic experience and his or her current difficulties. In this phase, the child learns to analyse responses to the trauma within the role of a scientist who analyses data (Kelly, 1955). The therapist here assists the traumatised child to analyse the process he or she underwent at a concrete, clear level according to his or her developmental abilities. The child learns to understand the progression from the frightening event experienced to the manner in which he or she reacted (aim 1).

Along with this new awareness during therapy, anxiety and fear can emerge due to children's perceptions of themselves as sick or crazy when they experience strange thoughts or have other than normal behaviour. Emphasis in this phase of the treatment should therefore be placed on the normalcy of the way the child thinks, feels, or acts in the circumstances and how such an event is expected to elicit the thoughts that brought out this kind of behaviour in the child, both at the time of the event and since that time. The child is taught about the human body's flight/fright and self-preservation mechanisms and about the relationship between the brain and the body, in a language appropriate to his or her developmental status. Thus therapeutic transformation begins with the development of the child's awareness of the *connection* between his or her interpretation and processing of the traumatic experience and his or her ongoing bodily, emotional, cognitive, and behavioural responses (aim 2). By gaining an understanding of their personal point of view and of how they reached the point of being traumatised, children are expected to accept the internal source of their responses and thereby the responsibility for their behaviour. Traumatised children often view their problems as produced by outside precipitators; therefore, they sense little if any control or hope of improvement, feeling that their difficulties are constant, everlasting, and impossible to change. A new explanation and new understanding of the situation can, in time, evoke the child's readiness to be changed (aim 3). For example, instead of recalling a circumstance in which 'I ran away', the child (after understanding the process) believes that his 'brain gave him an order to go', but now he can learn to intervene with such orders in the future.

Phase 3: Increasing awareness to internal stimuli

While learning to accept and understand behaviours and thoughts are difficult tasks, trying to become aware of internal sensations and to feel free to express emotions are even more difficult challenges for children. Many times children are trained, whether unintentionally or deliberately, to hide what they feel. In the previous phase, emphasis was placed on fostering children's understanding that their behaviours resulted from their feelings. This phase of the treatment model focuses on helping the child learn to become better acquainted with those feelings as manifested by internal messages sent by his or her own body (aim 1). Once the distressing internal cue is identified, along with its specific location, shape, and strength, it is related to emotions. Exercises such as 'being a scientist who studies behaviour' can be used in this phase to guide the child towards exploring these internal stimuli:

- What do you feel?
- When does the sensation occur?
- Where do you feel it?

- What does this mean to you?

For example, a girl who was in a traumatic automobile accident can thereby learn that the pains she feels in her stomach and her head make her 'very scared' and remind her of the accident. Children must be helped to differentiate each such sensation from other types of pain and to relate it to personal reasons:

- When do I feel this pain?
- Can it be a signal that I am afraid?
- Does it always appear at the same time, place, event?

The aforementioned girl may discover that whenever she is expected to enter a car, she gets a stomach ache, signalling that she is frightened of being involved in another crash (aim 2). Important gains are made when the child feels able to alter the texture of these ongoing bodily and emotional experiences. Next, the child can ask: What can I do in order to help the pain go away? Merely practising this identification process will enable the girl later on to dare trying to enter a car and ride in it (aim 3).

Phase 4: Developing self-control

After the child has examined and learned about his or her trauma, behaviour, and emotions (aim 1), it is time to start learning how to change the traumatic response. The child in this phase is likened to an architect (Kelly, 1955) who begins reconstructing his or her life by reconfiguring the meaning of the experience (aim 2) and by becoming empowered to grow out of the experience (aim 3). Significant progress in meaning-making occurs when the child feels able to experience himself or herself as more of an agent in his or her life stories.

The development of new meanings, constructs, and responses that will be more effective can be achieved using techniques such as guided imagination, writing assignments, role playing, and sculpturing. Imagination exercises could include: 'Imagine you are a superwoman who can do anything. What would you do?' or 'Let's take a trip to the future when your problem no longer exists. What do you look like? What is different?' or 'Watch a video of yourself in your mind and then use the remote control to change what needs to be changed. What would you change?' The therapist can use writing assignments such as: write a movie script and change its end and its meaning; imagine you are the movie director and cast yourself in the film, selecting the role in which you are most interested; write a book about your trauma; write a joke book about yourself, and so on. Role playing can help by letting the child be his or her own therapist, give a speech about himself or herself, try to make the event even more catastrophic, or try to make fun of himself or herself. Sculpturing techniques help the child to demonstrate the way he or she sees things: 'Use your family and build a sculpture which can symbolise your feelings, thoughts, or behaviours, and then change it.'

In addition to the aforementioned examples for techniques, children are very creative and have many ideas. The best method is to have every child invent his or her own techniques, taking ideas from personal experience and his or her own way of life. For instance, if a particular child is interested in art, the therapy can utilise art techniques; if another child loves computers, the therapy could focus on designing a computer program for change. The possibilities are limitless.

Phase 5: Eliminating the traumatised reaction

The last phase is reached as an achievement of all of the previous ones. Learning to give a new meaning to the traumatic event, to analyse one's undesired responses, to identify internal cues, and to act as an architect who confidently reconstrues one's life—all together culminate in the elimination of the traumatic reaction and the forging ahead of new ways of functioning (aims 1, 2, and 3 together). The child has allowed himself or herself to become exposed to the situation and memories which had previously been avoided. Thus, he or she can discover how to try facing a new reality that does not erase the trauma but rather includes it as an integral part of life, without devastating feelings or an inability to look toward the future.

Summary

In sum, the proposed cognitive–constructivist treatment for traumatised children is goal directed, with the intent to facilitate change in a challenging and empowering fashion. The child is an active partner who takes chances and is ready for new experiences. The therapist directs the treatment while being sensitive, creative, responsible for the new experiences, and suggestive. The methods, emphasising emotional and bodily sensations, are modified according to the child's areas of interest, readiness to participate, and willingness to enter into the adventure of change through metaphors and imagination.

Two case examples can illustrate the application of the model to traumatised children (Ronen, 1996b). Case example 1:

> A 10-year-old boy was referred to therapy with presenting symptoms of anxiety, fears, and avoidance behaviours. The parents claimed that he had been acting traumatised, although, to the best of their knowledge, he had never been exposed to what they considered a traumatic event. The child, on the other hand, claimed that all of his problems had begun since he got lost on a trip the family made abroad. He described the incident, relating his fear that he would never find his parents again. He had imagined himself being kidnapped or murdered by a stranger if he dared to ask for help in finding his way back. The boy also emphasised the large number of rapes and murders happening every day, and he drew a picture of a frightening stranger of whom he was afraid. The mother argued that he had never been lost, that this was only his imagination. Still, the child suffered from nightmares, a sleep disorder, experiences that resembled flashbacks, and bed-wetting. Whatever the external event that had occurred, the boy was traumatised by the experience.

> In therapy, during an exercise in supervised imagery, we took a trip to a foreign country, trying to experience what it felt like being left alone and to relive the situation of getting lost. We then acted out a role play where he played the part of his thoughts and I played the part of his emotions. Later on, while sitting in the 'therapist's chair', the boy attempted to help me look at the event as a challenging experience that tests one's sense of direction and the ability to speak a foreign language and adapt to a new environment. By the end of the session, he seemed to have learned to construe things differently, announcing that what he needed to do was learn from whom he could ask for help. He even exclaimed that maybe he should actually *try* to get lost next time because it seemed that it would be much less frightening than before, when he had just helplessly looked around for his parents. After a few more sessions, the nightmares ceased, as did the

sleep disorder and the enuresis. We terminated therapy by drawing a map for those who do not know that one can make the best out of the experience of getting lost, and we wrote a guide book with advice on how to find the way back to one's family in a foreign country.

Case example 2:

The second case example concerns an external event clearly defined as a trauma according to diagnostic criteria. A 6-year-old boy was referred to therapy after the murder of his father. The family had been living abroad for several years. During a visit with his mother to their country of origin, his father—still living abroad—was shot during a store robbery attempt. The mother, fearful of exposing her son to the traumatic event, told him that his father had been killed in a car accident and decided to move back with her son to their homeland. However, the boy found a newspaper with his father's picture and the whole story of the event. He was traumatised by the loss of his father but also felt insecure about his mother's untruth and the loss of his entire familiar environment (friends, home, school). He developed separation fears where he would not let his mother out of his sight. Feelings of guilt emerged about his responsibility for the event ('Maybe if I had been with Dad he would not have died'; 'He died without even seeing me for the last time'; 'We should have taken Dad with us on our trip', etc.). The child developed a sleep disorder, often cried, and became depressed, irritable, and nervous.

Therapy focused on helping the child 'as a scientist' to understand that there was nothing he could have done to prevent the occurrence of the murder, enabling him to change his guilt feelings. Through a process of meaning-making, the child was helped to reconstruct the event in a way he could understand (without the need to blame either himself or his father), live with it, and find ways to cherish memories from his life with his father. Using the metaphor of an architect, the child tried to design his new life in his new school with new friends, attempting to overcome his fears of being left alone or being murdered also. Through narrative and story-telling methods, he learned to accept his feelings, to expose himself to the memories of his father that he had earlier avoided, to cherish the past, and to try developing coping skills that would help him adapt himself to the new environment.

As his situation received a new interpretation (in terms of goals and steps towards change instead of deficiencies and problems in the child's functioning), the boy became very eager to change things and prove he could reach his goals. He practised role playing where he talked with his father, taking both parts of loving the father and missing him on the one hand and being angry at him for not being careful on the other hand. During many sessions he looked in the mirror, learning to accept his feelings, letting himself cry and be sad, and discovering which part of himself was present—the one that hated and was angry at the father or the part that missed and cared for him—and how he could shift from one part to the other. This therapy process could be termed both form-giving and meaning-making in its focus. The child practised writing a movie script, changing the end of the story, making his father a hero who survived, and later on making himself an adult who was not afraid of being exposed to the same event in which his father was killed.

GUIDELINES FOR THERAPISTS IN THE CLINICAL APPLICATION OF THE SELF-CONTROL INTERVENTION MODEL FOR CHILDREN

After assessment has pinpointed the need to treat the child individually, review the following points in your attempt to apply the self-control intervention model to children:

● Plan the first stage of the model—modification of maladaptive concepts. What concepts does the child demonstrate in relation to his or her disorder? How would you like these to be changed?
● For the second stage, how can you explain to the child the process of his or her presenting problem? Could you use metaphors? Painting? Reading materials?
● What programme would you design for increasing the child's sensitivity to internal stimuli (stage 3)?
● For the fourth stage, consider self-control exercises to be applied at school or home. What exercises could you ask the child to do?
● Could you assess the increase in confidence? Is the child acquiring observing and valuative skills? Do you see progress in elimination of the problem (stage 5)?

SUMMARY

The self-control model constitutes a combination of cognitive and behavioural techniques based on Rosenbaum's self-control model in conjunction with Beck's theoretical framework. Cognitive–behavioural therapy with children is a challenging intervention for the therapist. The outcomes demonstrated up to the present time are not yet sufficient, but already the possible advantages children could gain from such forms of intervention are evident. In the short run, children can learn to become able to solve their own problems, fostering their sense of empowerment; moreover, in the long run, such a treatment paradigm seems to enable children to generate other solutions, generalising the learned skills in order to prevent future problems.

15

EPILOGUE: CONCLUSIONS AND FUTURE DIRECTIONS

The future of child cognitive-behavioural therapy lies in the ability of researchers and clinicians to adapt their work to children's specific needs. First, there is a strong necessity to design a comprehensive theory incorporating assessment of the child's problem, intervention, and evaluation of the treatment's efficacy within the context of the same therapeutic mode. A discrepancy often exists between assessment and intervention, where, following a standard assessment process, therapists usually rely on applications of different techniques to determine what actually helps. Only through their ability to design an assessment mode that inherently points to the kind of intervention needed will therapists be able to provide an appropriate answer to each child's problem.

Second, cognitive-behavioural therapists working with children should add knowledge of developmental and social psychology to their knowledge of the behavioural and cognitive realms. An integration of knowledge bases would precipitate the modification of the appropriate model to the individual child's developmental status in cognitive, emotional, and motor areas.

Third, there is a need to continue our study on the efficacy of children's treatments, while weighing several features: the child's natural environment and its specific needs; the capability of the child, and the nature of the problem. These three considerations will equip the therapist to answer the following question: *What is the best intervention mode for this specific child, in light of his or her developmental needs, the presented problem, and the environmental conditions?* Different children, at different ages and socio-economic status levels, need different kinds of intervention.

Fourth, most of the widely-used child techniques constitute a direct adaptation of adult techniques. The inadequacy of these techniques to attend to children's specific behaviour problems and to their developmental abilities strongly calls for the development of specific techniques for children that purposefully address two unique features: children's irrational thinking and their need for a sense of enjoyment from the subject at hand. These characteristics necessitate a flexibility in therapeutic modes, to include painting, imagery, and psychodrama.

Fifth, most available therapies, especially for children, are directed towards existing problems. Designing interventions that target prevention can help facilitate children's general adjustment and coping.

And last, but not least, behavioural therapy strongly highlights positive forces and empowerment. Until recently, most therapies were directed towards problems and overcoming them. Adult therapy nowadays includes techniques for teaching people to be happy, opening up to experiences, and letting go of problems (Mahoney, 1990). Concentrating interventions on opening up to experiences from an early age may contribute towards the maturation of a generation which can improve their quality of life, enjoy new experiences, and focus on happiness rather than on difficulties and sorrows.

REFERENCES

Achenbach, T. M. (1985). *Assessment and taxonomy of child and adolescent psychopathology*. Beverly Hills, CA: Sage.

Achenbach, T. M. (1993). Implications of multiaxial empirically based assessment for behavior therapy with children. *Behavior Therapy, 24*, 91–116.

Akhtar, N. & Bradley, E. J. (1991). Social information processing deficits of aggressive children: Present findings and implications for social skills training. *Clinical Psychology Review, 11*, 621–644.

American Psychiatric Association (1994). *Diagnostic and statistical manual of mental disorders* (4th edn). Washington, DC: Author.

Angold, A., Weissman, M., Merikangas, J. K., Prusoff, B., Wickramaratne, P., Gammon, G., & Warner, B. (1987). Parent and child reports of depressive symptoms in children at low and high risk of depression. *Journal of Child Psychology and Psychiatry, 28*, 901–915.

Azrin, N. H. & Nunn, R. G. (1974). A rapid method of eliminating stuttering by a regulated breathing approach. *Behaviour Research and Therapy, 8*, 3–33.

Baer, D. M. (1985). Applied behavior analysis as a conceptually conservative view of childhood disorders. In R. J. McMahon & R. DeV. Peters (Eds), *Childhood disorders: Behavioral developmental approaches* (pp. 17–35). New York: Bruner/Mazel.

Bandura, A. (1969). *Principles of behavior modification*. New York: Holt, Rinehart & Winston.

Bandura, A. (1977). *Social learning theory*. Englewood Cliffs, NJ: Prentice Hall.

Baron, P. & Peixoto, N. (1991). Depressive symptoms in adolescents as a function of personality factors. *Journal of Youth and Adolescence, 20*, 493–500.

Barrios, B. A. & Harmann, D. P. (1988). Fears and anxieties. In E. J. Mash & L. G. Terdal (Eds), *Behavioral assessment of childhood disorders* (2nd edn, pp. 196–262). New York: Guilford.

Beck, A. T. (1963). Thinking and depression. *Archives of General Psychiatry, 9*, 324–333.

Beck, A. T. (1976). *Cognitive therapy and the emotional disorders.* New York: Meridian.

Beck, A. T., Emery, G., & Greenberg, R. L. (1985). *Anxiety disorders and phobias.* New York: Basic Books.

Beck, A. T., Freeman, A., & Associates (1990). *Cognitive therapy of personality disorders.* New York: Guilford.

Beck, A. T., Rush, A. J., Shaw, B. F., & Emery, G. (1979). *Cognitive therapy of depression.* New York: Guilford.

Beidel, D. C. & Turner, S. M. (1986). A critique of the theoretical bases of cognitive-behavioural theories and therapy. *Clinical Psychology Review,* **6**, 177–197.

Belter, R. W., Dunn, S. E., & Jeney, P. (1991). The psychological impact of Hurricane Hugo on children: A needs assessment. *Advance of Behavior Research & Therapy,* **13**, 155–161.

Bergin, A. E. & Garfield, S. L. (1994). *Handbook of psychotherapy and behavior change* (4th edn). New York: Wiley.

Bierman, K. L. & Furman, W. (1984). The effects of social skills training and peer involvement on the social adjustment of preadolescents. *Child Development,* **55**, 151–162.

Bornstein, M., Bellack, A. S., & Hersen, M. (1977). Social skills training for unassertive children: A multiple-baseline analysis. *Journal of Applied Behavior Analysis,* **10**, 183–195.

Brandell, J. R. (1992). Psychotherapy of a traumatized 10-year-old boy: Theoretical issues and clinical considerations. *Smith College Studies in Social Work,* **62**, 123–138.

Brigham, T. A., Hopper, C., Hill, B., Armas, A. D. & Newsom, P. (1985). A self-management program for disruptive adolescents in the school: A clinical replication in analysis. *Behaviour Therapy,* **16**, 99–115.

Brown, R. T., Borden, K. A., Wynne, M. E., Schleser, R., & Clingerman, S. R. (1986). Methylphenidate and cognitive therapy with ADD children: A methodological reconsideration. *Journal of Abnormal Child Psychology,* **14**, 481–497.

Campbell, S. (1990). *Behavior problems in preschool children.* New York: Guilford.

Cartledge, G. & Milburn, J. F. (1986). *Teaching social skills to children: Innovative approach.* New York: Pergamon.

Casey, R. J. & Berman, J. S. (1985). The outcome of psychotherapy with children. *Psychological Bulletin,* **98**, 388–400.

Coats, K. I. (1979). Cognitive self-instructional training approach for reducing disruptive behavior of young children. *Psychological Reports,* **44**, 127–134.

Copeland, A. P. (1982). Individual difference factors in children's self-management: Toward individualized treatment. In P. Karoly & F. H.

Kanfer (Eds), *Self-management and behavior change: From theory to practice* (pp. 207–239). New York: Pergamon.

Cowen, E. L. (1980). The wooing of primary prevention strategy. *American Journal of Community Psychology,* **8**, 258–284.

Craighead, W. E., Meyer, A. W., & Craighead, L. W. (1985). A conceptual model for cognitive behavior therapy with children. *Journal of Abnormal Child Psychology,* **13**, 331–342.

Crick, N. R. & Dodge, K. A. (1994). A review and reformulation of social information-processing mechanisms in children's social adjustment. *Psychological Bulletin,* **115**, 74–101.

Doleys, D. M. (1977). Behavioral treatments for nocturnal enuresis in children: A review of the recent literature. *Psychological Bulletin,* **84**, 30–54.

Douglas, V. I. (1972). Stop, look and listen: The problem of sustained attention and impulse control in hyperactive and normal children. *Canadian Journal of Behavioral Science,* **4**, 259–282.

Durlak, J. A., Fuhrman, T., & Lampman, C. (1991). Effectiveness of cognitive-behavior therapy for maladaptive children: A meta-analysis. *Psychological Bulletin,* **110**, 204–214.

Dush, D. M., Hirt, M. L., & Schroeder, H. E. (1989). Self-statement modification in the treatment of child behavior disorders: A meta-analysis. *Psychological Bulletin,* **106**, 97–106.

Elias, M. J., Gara, M., Ubriaco, M., Rothbaum, P., Clabby, J. F., & Schuyler, T. (1986). Impact of a preventive social problem solving intervention on children's coping with middle stressors. *American Journal of Community Psychology,* **14**, 259–275.

Ellis, A. (1958). Rational psychotherapy. *Journal of General Psychology,* **59**, 35–49.

Ellis, A. (1962). *Reason and emotion in psychotherapy.* New York: Lyle Stuart.

Eysenck, H. J. (1959). Learning theory and behavior therapy. *Journal of Mental Science,* **105**, 61–75.

Fielding, D. M. (1980). The response of day and night wetting children and children who wet only at night to retention control training and the enuresis alarm. *Behaviour Research and Therapy,* **18**, 305–317.

Fielding, D. M. (1982). An analysis of the behavior of day and night wetting children: Towards a model of micturition control. *Behaviour Research and Therapy,* **20**, 49–60.

Finch, A. J., Nelson, W. M., & Ott, E. S. (1993). *Cognitive-behavioral procedures with children and adolescents: A practical guide.* Boston: Allyn & Bacon.

Finch, A. J., Wilkinson, M. D., Nelson, W. M., & Montgomery, L. E. (1975). Modification of impulsive cognitive tempo in emotionally disturbed boys. *Journal of Abnormal Child Psychology,* **13**, 49–52.

Fleming, C. C. (1982). Evaluation of an anger management program with aggressive children in residential treatment. *Dissertation Abstracts International*, **43**, 4143B.

Forehand, R. & Weirson, M. (1993). The role of developmental factors in planning behavioral intervention for children: Disruptive behavior as an example. *Behavior Therapy*, **24**, 117–141.

Forman, S. G. (1980). A comparison of cognitive training and response cost procedures in modifying aggressive behavior of elementary school children. *Behavior Therapy*, **11**, 594–600.

Gambrill, E. (1990). *Critical thinking in clinical practice*. San Francisco: Jossey-Bass.

Garfield, S. L. (1983). Effectiveness of psychotherapy: The perennial controversy. *Professional Psychology*, **14**, 35–43.

Gelfand, D. M. & Hartman, D. P. (1984). *Child behavior analysis and therapy*. New York: Pergamon.

Gorton, M. V. (1985). The efficacy of teaching social skills to socially isolated preadolescents. *Dissertation Abstracts International*, **47**, 4328B.

Graziano, A. M. (1978). Behavior therapy. In B. B. Wolman & A. O. Ross (Eds), *Handbook of treatment of mental disorders in childhood and adolescence*. Englewood Cliffs, NJ: Prentice Hall.

Graziano, A. M., Mooney, K. C., Hurber, C., & Ignasiak, D. (1979). Self-control instruction for children's fear-reduction. *Journal of Behavior Therapy and Experimental Psychology*, **10**, 221–227.

Gresham, F. M. (1981). Social skills training with handicapped children: A review. *Review of Educational Research*, **51**, 139–176.

Gresham, F. M. & Nagle, R. J. (1980). Social skills training with children: Responsiveness to modeling and coaching as a function of peer orientation. *Journal of Consulting and Clinical Psychology*, **48**, 718–729.

Gross, A. M. & Drabman, R. S. (1982). Teaching self-recording, self-evaluation, and self-reward to non-clinic children and adolescents. In P. K. Karoly & F. H. Kanfer (Eds), *Self-management and behavior change: From theory to practice* (pp. 285–314). New York: Pergamon.

Hallman, N. (1950). On the ability of enuretic children to hold urine. *Acta Pediatrica*, **39**, 87.

Harris, K. R. & Brown, R. D. (1982). Cognitive-behaviour modification and informed teacher treatments for shy children. *Journal of Experimental Education*, **50**, 137–143.

Hartman, D. P. & Wood, D. D. (1982). Observational methods. In A. S. Pollack, M. Hersen, & A. E. Kazdin (Eds), *International handbook of behavior modification and therapy* (pp. 109–138). New York: Plenum.

Hersen, M. & Van Hasselt, V. B. (Eds) (1987). *Behavior therapy with children and adolescents*. New York: Wiley.

Hodges, K., Gordon, Y., & Lennon, M. P. (1990). Parent–child agreement on symptoms assessed via clinical research interview for children: The child assessment schedule (CAS). *Journal of Child Psychiatry*, **31**, 427–436.

Hollon, S. D. & Beck, A. T. (1994). Cognitive and cognitive behavioral therapies. In A. E. Bergin & S. L. Garfield (Eds), *Handbook of psychotherapy and behavior change* (4th edn, pp. 428–466). New York: Wiley.

Hughes, J. N. (1988). *Cognitive behavior therapy with children in schools*. New York: Pergamon.

Hughes, J. N. (1993). Behavior therapy. In T. R. Kratochwill & R. J. Morris (Eds), *Handbook of psychotherapy with children and adolescents* (pp. 185–220). Boston: Allyn & Bacon.

Jackson, H. J. & King, N. J. (1981). The emotive imagery treatment of a child's trauma-induced phobia. *Journal of Behavior Therapy and Experiential Psychiatry*, **12**, 325–328.

Jacobson, E. (1938). *Progressive relaxation*. Chicago: University of Chicago.

Kanfer, F. H. (1970). Self-regulation: Research, issues, and speculations. In C. Neuringer & J. L. Michael (Eds), *Behavior modifications in clinical psychology* (pp. 178–220). New York: Appleton Century Crofts.

Kanfer, F. H. (1977). The many faces of self-control, or behavior modification changes its focus. In R. B. Stuart (Ed.), *Behavioral self-management* (pp. 1–48). New York: Brunner/Mazel.

Kanfer, F. H., Karoly, P., & Newman, P. (1975). Reduction of children's fear of dark by competence-related and situational threat-related verbal cues. *Journal of Consulting and Clinical Psychology*, **43**, 251–258.

Kanfer, F. H. & Philips, J. S. (1970). *Learning foundation of behavior therapy*. New York: Wiley.

Kanfer, F. H. & Schefft, B. K. (1988). *Guiding the process of therapeutic change*. Champaign, IL: Research.

Karoly, P. & Jensen, M. P. (1987). *Multimethod assessment of chronic pain*. New York: Pergamon.

Karoly, P. & Kanfer, F. H. (Eds) (1982). *Self-management and behavior change: From theory to practice*. New York: Pergamon.

Kaslow, N. J., Rhem, L. P., Pollack, S. L., & Siegal, W. (1988). Attributional style and self-control behavior in depressed and nondepressed children and their parents. *Journal of Abnormal Child Psychology*, **16**, 163–175.

Kazdin, A. E. (1979). Advances in child behavior therapy. In S. I. Pfeiffer (Ed.), *Clinical child psychology: Introduction to theory, research and practice*. Orlando, FL: Grune & Stratton.

Kazdin, A. E. (1982). *Single-case research design: Methods for clinical and applied settings*. New York: Oxford University.

Kazdin, A. E. (1986). The evaluation of psychotherapy: Research design and methodology. In S. L. Garfield & A. E. Bergin (Eds), *Handbook of psychotherapy and behavior change* (3rd edn, pp. 23–68). New York: Wiley.

REFERENCES

Kazdin, A. E. (1987). *Conduct disorders in childhood and au* bury Park, CA: Sage.

Kazdin, A. E. (1988). *Child psychotherapy: Development and idu tive treatments.* New York: Pergamon.

Kazdin, A. E. (1994). Psychotherapy for children and adolescei Bergin & S. L. Garfield (Eds), *Handbook of psychotherapy and benu. change* (4th edn, pp. 543–594). New York: Wiley.

Kazdin, A. E., Esveldt-Dawson, K., French, N. H., & Unis, A. S. (1987). Problem solving skills training and relationship therapy in the treatment of antisocial child behavior. *Journal of Consulting and Clinical Psychology,* **55**, 76–85.

Kelly, G. A. (1955). *The psychology of personal constructs.* New York: Norton.

Kendall, P. C. (1993). Cognitive-behavioral therapies with youth: Guiding theory, current status, and emerging developments. *Journal of Consulting and Clinical Psychology,* **61**, 235–247.

Kendall, P. C. (1994). Treating anxiety disorders in youth: Results of a randomized clinical trial. *Journal of Consulting and Clinical Psychology,* **62**, 100–110.

Kendall, P. C. & Braswell, L. (1982). Cognitive-behavioral assessment: Model, measures, and madness. In J. N. Butcher & C. D. Spielberger (Eds), *Advances in personality assessment* (Vol. 1, pp. 35–82). Hillsdale, NJ: Erlbaum.

Kendall, P. C. & Braswell, L. (1985). *Cognitive-behavioral therapy for impulsive children.* New York: Guilford.

Kendall, P. C. & Finch, A. J. (1979). Analysis of changes in verbal behavior following a cognitive-behavioral treatment for impulsivity. *Journal of Abnormal Child Psychology,* **7**, 455–463.

Kendall, P. C. & Hollon, S. D. (1979) (Eds). *Cognitive-behavioural interventions: Theory, research, and procedures.* New York: Academic Press.

Kendall, P. C. & Morris, R. J. (1991). Child therapy: Issues and recommendations. *Journal of Consulting and Clinical Psychology,* **59**, 777–784.

Kendall, P. C., Reber, M., McLeer, S., Epps, J., & Ronan, K. R. (1990). Cognitive-behavioral treatment of conduct-disordered children. *Cognitive Therapy and Research,* **14**, 279–297.

Kendall, P. C., Stark, K. D., & Adam, T. (1990). Cognitive deficit or cognitive distortion in children's depression. *Journal of Abnormal Child Psychology,* **18**, 255–270.

Kendall, P. C. & Wilcox, L. E. (1980). Cognitive-behavioral treatment for impulsivity: Concrete versus conceptual training in non-self-controlled problem children. *Journal of Consulting and Clinical Psychology,* **48**, 80–91.

Kessler, J. (1966). *Psychopathology of childhood.* Englewood Cliffs, NJ: Prentice Hall.

King, N., Hamilton, D., & Ollendick, T. (1988). *Children's phobias: A behavioral perspective*. New York: Wiley.

Kingsley, G. J. (1987). The efficacy of a self-instruction attribution retraining program in alleviating learned helplessness and depressive symptomatology in learning disabled children. *Dissertation Abstracts International*, **48**, 879B.

Knell, S. M. (1993). *Cognitive behavioral play therapy*, Northvale: Aronson.

Koeppen, A. S. (1974). Relaxation training for children. *Elementary School Guidance and Counseling*, **9**, 14–21.

Kratochwill, T. R. & Morris, R. J. (1991). *The practice of child psychotherapy* (2nd ed.). New York: Pergamon.

Kratochwill, T. R. & Morris, R. J. (1993). *Handbook of psychotherapy with children and adolescents*. Boston: Allyn & Bacon.

Lapouse, R. & Monk, M. A. (1958). An epidemiologic study of behavior characteristics in children. *American Journal of Public Health*, **48**, 1134–1144.

Lazarus, A. A. (1960). The elimination of children's phobias by deconditioning. In H. J. Eysenck (Ed.), *Behavior therapy and the neuroses* (pp. 114–122). Oxford: Pergamon.

Levitt, E. E. (1963). Psychotherapy with children: A further evaluation. *Behavior Research and Therapy*, **60**, 326–329.

Lochman, J. E., Burch, P. P., Curry, F. J., & Lampron, L. B. (1984). Treatment and generalization effects of cognitive-behavioral and goal-setting interventions with aggressive boys. *Journal of Consulting and Clinical Psychology*, **52**, 915–916.

Lochman, J. E., Nelson, W. M., III, & Sims, J. P. (1981). A cognitive behavioral program for use with aggressive children. *Journal of Clinical Child Psychology*, **10**, 146–148.

Lovaas, O. I. (1967). A behavior therapy approach to the treatment of childhood schizophrenia. In J. P. Hill (Ed.), *Minnesota Symposium on child psychology*. Minneapolis: University of Minnesota.

Luria, A. R. (1961). *The role of speech in the regulation of normal behaviors*. New York: Liverwright.

Mahoney, M. J. (1977). Reflections on the cognitive learning trend in psychotherapy. *American Psychologist*, **32**, 5–13.

Mahoney, M. J. (1991). *Human change processes*. New York: Basic Books.

Magg, J. & Kotlash, J. (1994). Review of stress inoculation training with children and adolescents. *Behavior Modification*, **18**, 443–470.

Marks, I. (1969). *Fears and phobias*. New York: Academic Press.

Marks, I. (1978). *Living with fear*. New York: McGraw-Hill.

Marks, I. (1987). *Fears, phobias and rituals*. New York: Oxford University.

Marlatt, G. A. & Parks, G. A. (1982). Self-management of addictive disorders. In P. Karoly & F. H. Kanfer (Eds), *Self-management and behavior change: From theory to practice* (pp. 443–488). New York: Pergamon.

Mash, E. & Terdal, L. G. (1988). Behavioral assessment of child and family disturbance. In E. J. Mash & L. G. Terdal (Eds), *Behavioral assessment of childhood disorders* (2nd edn, pp. 3–69). New York: Guilford.

Mathews, A. M., Gelder, M. G., & Johnston, D. W. (1981). *Agoraphobia: Nature and treatment.* New York: Guilford.

McMahon, R. J. & Peters, R. DeV. (Eds) (1985). *Childhood disorders: Behavioral developmental approaches.* New York: Bruner/Mazel.

Meichenbaum, D. H. (1979). Teaching children self-control. In B. Lahey & A. Kazdin (Eds), *Advances in clinical child psychology* (Vol. 2, pp. 1–30). New York: Plenum.

Meichenbaum, D. H. (1985). *Stress inoculation training.* New York: Pergamon.

Meichenbaum, D. H., Bream, L. A., & Cohen, J. S. (1985). A cognitive-behavioral perspective of child psychopathology: Implications for assessment and training. In R. J. McMahon & R. DeV. Peters (Eds), *Childhood disorders: Behavioral developmental approaches* (pp. 36–52). New York: Bruner/Mazel.

Meichenbaum, D. H. & Goodman, J. (1971). Training impulsive children to talk to themselves: A means of developing self-control. *Journal of Abnormal Psychology, 77,* 115–126.

Meichenbaum, D. H. & Turk, D. C. (1987). *Facilitating treatment adherence: A practitioner's guidebook.* New York: Plenum.

Miller, S. H. (1979). Controllability and human stress: Method, evidence and theory. *Behaviour Research and Therapy, 12,* 287–304.

Mischel, W. (1973). Toward a cognitive social learning reconceptualization of personality. *Psychological Review, 80,* 252–283.

Mischel, W. (1974). Processes in delay of gratifications. In L. Berkowitz (Ed.), *Advances in experimental and social psychology.* New York: Academic Press.

Montenegro, H. (1968). Severe separation anxiety in two preschool children: Successfully treated by reciprocal inhibition. *Journal of Child Psychology and Psychiatry, 9,* 93–103.

Morris, R. J. & Kratochwill, T. R. (1983). *Treating children's fears and phobias: A behavioral approach.* New York: Pergamon.

Morris, R. J. & Kratochwill, T. R. (1991). Childhood fears and phobias. In T. R. Kratochwill & R. J. Morris (Eds), *The practice of child therapy* (pp. 76–114). New York: Pergamon.

Novaco, R. W. (1979). The cognitive regulation of anger and stress. In P. C. Kendall & S. E. Hollon (Eds), *Cognitive-behavioral interventions: Theory, research and practice* (pp. 241–285). New York: Academic Press.

O'Connor, R. D. (1972). Relative efficacy of modeling, shaping and the combined procedures for modification of social withdrawal. *Journal of Abnormal Psychology, 79,* 327–334.

Ollendick, T. H. & Cerny, J. A. (1981). *Clinical behavior therapy with children.* New York: Plenum.

Ost, L. G., Salkovskis, P. M., & Hellstrom, K. (1991). One-session therapist-directed exposure vs. self-exposure in the treatment of spider phobia. *Behavior Therapy*, **22**, 407–422.

Paul, G. L. (1967). Outcome research in psychotherapy. *Journal of Consulting Psychology*, **31**, 109–118.

Piaget, J. (1926). *The language and thought of the child.* London: Routledge & Kegan Paul.

Powell, M. B. & Oei, T. P. S. (1991). Cognitive processes underlying the behavior change in cognitive behavior therapy with childhood disorders: A review of experimental evidence. *Behavioural Psychotherapy*, **19**, 247–265.

Reid, J. B., Kavanagh, K., & Baldwin, D. (1987). Abusive parents' perceptions of child problem behaviors: An example of parental bias. *Journal of Abnormal Child Psychiatry*, **15**, 457–466.

Reid, W. (1978). *The task centered system.* New York: Columbia University.

Rhem, L. P. (1977). A self-control model of depression. *Behavior Therapy*, **8**, 787–804.

Reynolds, W. M. & Coats, K. I. (1986). A comparison of cognitive–behavioral therapy and relaxation training for the treatment of depression in adolescents. *Journal of Consulting and Clinical Psychology*, **54**, 653–660.

Robin, A. L. (1985). Parent–adolescent conflict: A developmental problem of families. In R. J. McMahon & R. DeV. Peters (Eds), *Childhood disorders: Behavioral developmental approaches* (pp. 244–265). New York: Bruner/Mazel.

Ronen, T. (1991). Intervention package for treating sleep disorders in a four-year-old girl. *Behavior Therapy and Experimental Psychiatry*, **22**, 141–148.

Ronen, T. (1992). Cognitive therapy with young children. *Child Psychiatry and Human Development*, **23**, 19–30.

Ronen, T. (1993a). Adapting treatment techniques to children's needs. *British Journal of Social Work*, **23**, 581–596.

Ronen, T. (1993b). Decision making about children's therapy. *Child Psychiatry and Human Development*, **23**, 259–272.

Ronen, T. (1993c). Intervention package for treating encopresis in a 6 year old boy: A case study. *Behavioural Psychotherapy*, **21**, 127–135.

Ronen, T. (1993d). Self-control training in the treatment of sleep terror disorder: A case study. *Child and Family Behavior Therapy*, **15**, 53–63.

Ronen, T. (1994a). *And most of all love: Skills and art in child therapy.* Tel Aviv: Ramot (Hebrew).

Ronen, T. (1994b). Imparting self-control in the school setting. *Child and Family Behavior Therapy*, **16**, 1–20.

Ronen, T. (1995). From what kind of self-control can children benefit? *Journal of Cognitive Psychotherapy: An International Quarterly*, **9**, 45–61.

Ronen, T. (1996a). Constructivist therapy with traumatised children. *The Journal of Constructivism*, **9**, 139–156.

Ronen, T. (1996b). Self-control exposure therapy for treating children's anxieties. *Child and Family Behavior Therapy*, **18**, 1–17.

Ronen, T. & Abraham, Y. (1995). The relative efficacy of retention control training (RCT) for the treatment of younger versus older enuretic children. *Nursing Research*, **45**, 78–82.

Ronen, T., Rahav, G., & Wozner, Y. (1995). Self-control and enuresis. *Journal of Cognitive Psychotherapy: An International Quarterly*, **9**, 249–258.

Ronen, T. & Wozner, Y. (1995). A self-control intervention package for the treatment of primary nocturnal enuresis. *Child and Family Behavior Therapy*, **17**, 1–20.

Ronen, T., Wozner, Y., & Rahav, G. (1992). Cognitive intervention in enuresis. *Child and Family Behavior Therapy*, **14**, 1–20.

Rose, S. D. & Edelson, J. L. (1988). *Working with children and adolescents in groups*. San Francisco: Jossey-Bass.

Rosenbaum, M. (1990). The role of learned resourcefulness in self-control of health behavior. In M. Rosenbaum (Ed.), *Learned resourcefulness: On coping skills, self-control and adaptive behavior* (pp. 3–30). New York: Springer.

Rosenbaum, M. (1993). The three functions of self-control behavior: Redressive, reformative and experiential. *Journal of Work and Stress*, **7**, 33–46.

Rosenbaum, M. (in press). The self-regulation of experience: Openness and constructions. In P. Dewe, T. Cox, & A. M. Leiter (Eds), *Coping and health in organizations*. London: Taylor & Francis.

Rossman, B. B. R. (1992). School-age children's perceptions of coping with distress: Strategies for emotion regulation and moderation of adjustment. *Journal of Child Psychology and Psychiatry and Allied Disciplines*, **33**, 1373–1397.

Rychlak, J. F. (1968). *A philosophy of science for personality theory*. Boston: Houghton Mifflin.

Safran, J. D. & Segal, Z. V. (1990). *Interpersonal process in cognitive therapy*. New York: Basic Books.

Sahler, O. J. Z. & McAnarney, E. R. (1981). *The child from three to eighteen*. London: Mosby.

Schaffer, H. R. (1990). *Making decisions about children: Psychology questions and answers*. Oxford: Basil Blackwell.

Shein, S., Ronen, T., & Israelshvilly, M. (1995). *The influence of infant schooling in personality variables: Self-control, learning self-efficacy and state anxiety of a child before and after the transition to first grade*. Unpublished master's thesis, Tel Aviv University, Tel Aviv, Israel.

Sheldon, B. (1987). Implementing findings from social work effectiveness research. *British Journal of Social Work,* **17**, 573–586.

Spivack, G. & Shure, M. B. (1974). *Social adjustment of young children: A cognitive approach to solving real-life problems.* San Francisco: Jossey-Bass.

Stein, J. & Gambrill, E. (1977). Facilitating decision making in foster care. *Social Service Review,* **51**, 502–511.

Stuart, R. B. & Tripodi, T. (1973). Experimental evaluation of three time constrained behavioural treatments for pre-delinquents. In R. D. Rubin (Ed.), *Advances in behavior therapy.*

Tasto, D. L. (1969). Systematic desensitization, muscle relaxation and visual imagery in the counter-conditioning of a four-year-old phobic child. *Behaviour Research and Therapy,* **7**, 409–411.

Taylor, D. W. (1972). Treatment of excessive frequency of urination by desensitization. *Journal of Behavior Therapy and Experimental Psychiatry,* **3**, 311–313.

Thoresen, C. E. & Mahoney, M. J. (1974). *Behavioral self-control.* New York: Holt, Rinehart & Winston.

Vaal, J. J. (1973). Applying contingency contracting to a school phobic: A case study. *Journal of Behavior Therapy and Experimental Psychiatry,* **4**, 371–373.

Vygotsky, L. (1962). *Thought and language.* New York: Wiley.

Weisz, J. R., Weiss, B., Alicke, M. D., & Klotz, M. L. (1987). Effectiveness of psychotherapy with children and adolescence: A meta-analysis for clinician. *Journal of Consulting and Clinical Psychology,* **55**, 542–549.

Wenar, C. (1982). Developmental psychopathology: Its nature and models. *Journal of Clinical Child Psychology,* **11**, 192–201.

Whalen, C. K., Henker, B., & Hinshaw, S. P. (1985). Cognitive–behavioral therapies for hyperactive children: Premises, problems, and prospects. *Journal of Abnormal Child Psychology,* **13**, 319–410.

Wolman, B. B. (1982). *Children's fears.* Tel Aviv: Zmora Bitan, Modan (Hebrew).

Wolpe, J. (1982). *The practice of behavior therapy* (3rd edn). New York: Pergamon.

Wozner, Y. (1985). *Behavior change.* Tel Aviv: Papyrus (Hebrew).

Yule, W. (1990). The effect of disasters on children. *Bereavement Care,* **9**, 2–5.

INDEX

Index compiled by Alan Whittle

Related titles of interest from Wiley...

Understanding and Teaching Children with Autism

Rita Jordan and Stuart D. Powell

Addresses the fundamental problems of autism - relationships, communication and flexibility of thought and behaviour.

0-471-95888-3 188pp 1995 Hardback
0-471-95714-3 188pp 1995 Paperback

Culture and the Child

A Guide for Professionals in Child Care and Development

Daphne Keats

A handy practical guide for those professionals dealing with children whose cultural backgrounds differ from those of the mainstream of the society in which they live.

0-471-96625-8 160pp 1997 Paperback

Women Who Sexually Abuse Children

From Research to Clinical Practice

Jacqui Saradjian in association with Helga Hanks

Provides information on the ways in which women can and do sexually abuse.

Wiley Series in Child Care & Protection
0-471-96072-1   336pp   1996   Paperback

The Emotionally Abused and Neglected Child

Identification, Assessment and Intervention

Dorota Iwaniec

Explores the definition, identification and treatment of the difficult problem of emotional abuse.

Wiley Series in Child Care & Protection
0-471-95579-5 222pp 1995 Paperback

Visit the Wiley Home Page at http://www.wiley.co.uk